POLITICAL CORRUPTION

In

BRIDGEPORT

SCANDAL
in the
Park City

ROB SULLIVAN

Charleston · London

THE
History
PRESS

Published by The History Press
Charleston, SC 29403
www.historypress.net

Copyright © 2014 by Rob Sullivan
All rights reserved

Cover photos courtesy of the Bridgeport History Center, Bridgeport Public Library.

First published 2014

Manufactured in the United States

ISBN 978.1.62619.230.0

Library of Congress CIP data applied for.

To Gerri Whitlock,
without whose friendship and guidance this book would never have been written,

and to the memory of my parents,
John and Marilyn Sullivan.

CONTENTS

ACKNOWLEDGEMENTS

In the research and writing of this book, I have been fortunate to have had a great time and a wonderful experience, neither of which would have happened without a countless number of caring and talented people.

First and foremost is the outstanding crew at the Bridgeport History Center, the jewel of the Bridgeport Public Library. Mary Witkowski, Elizabeth Van Tuyl and Robert Jeffries are the reason you are reading this book. Without their help, this attempt at re-creating Bridgeport's political history would have been futile.

Speaking of the Bridgeport Public Library, another person without whom this work would not exist is Michael Bielawa, longtime library employee and fellow writer. Mike graciously listened to my idea for a book about Bridgeport politics and put me in contact with the good folks at The History Press. I still owe him a trip to a Brooklyn Cyclones baseball game for his kindness.

My commissioning editors Mattie Sowash and Tabitha Dulla and project editor Julia Turner have been a joy to work with, and I would also like to thank their predecessor, Jeff Saraceno, who brought this idea to the powers that be.

There have been countless friends and supporters who have been wonderful to me, and I have undoubtedly omitted more than a few, for which I apologize. However, here are a few more who have been a great help: Kathleen Maher, executive director of the Barnum Museum, took a lot of time to educate me about the great P.T.; John Whitlock chipped in with a great deal of support; and my sisters, June Eressy and Nancy Buniowski, and

ACKNOWLEDGEMENTS

their families, as well as my late brother, Jack Sullivan. Michael Murren of Murren Insurance was gracious enough to let me use his office whenever I needed it. Mr. Jim Fitzpatrick of Fairfield University has been an inspiration, as have many of my classmates from long ago, especially two who are no longer with us, Joe Graziano and Chris Eaton.

Of those who are no longer with us, my late politics professor, Dr. John Orman, helped stoke my love of politics during the many classes I took from him.

In Bridgeport politics, this generation's man for all seasons is undoubtedly Lennie Grimaldi, who has been through all facets of life at Bridgeport City Hall. From ace journalist to administration honcho to political power broker to—well, just read the book and find out. Speaking of reading the book, please check out the bibliography. Among other nuggets, you will find there the men and women who graciously gave up their time to allow me an interview. I am grateful to all of them, and I sincerely appreciate their kindness and their knowledge.

Again in terms of Park City politics, it was a subject I knew almost nothing about when I arrived here in 1996. I got a quick working knowledge on this fascinating subject, and here is an incomplete list of some of my mentors who pointed me in the right direction: Brad Durrell, Sean D'Arcy Danny Roach, George Ganim Sr., Joan Magnuson, Starlight, Mike Meehan, Bob Fredericks, Jim Clark, Mike Giannotti, Tom Mulligan, Tom Lombard, Hector Diaz, Lee Samowitz, George Comer, Barry Piesner, Todd Burger and Rich DeParle.

Writers require an abundance of food and drink, and to that end, I would like to express my appreciation to the owners and patrons of such fantastic Bridgeport eateries as Matty's Corner, Take Time Café, Amici Mici, Harborview Market, Two Boots, Murphy's Law, Ralph 'n Rich's, Ray Kelly's, Firehouse Pizza, Nick's Grocery, Taco Loco, Beverly Pizza and many more. Thanks for the calories!

Finally, I would especially like to thank all the Bridgeport politicians who have graced the Park City through the years. Good and bad, tall and short, fat and skinny—they have come in all shapes and sizes, and they have all been colorful characters. And for all their flaws and foibles, the political dynamos that grace these pages are simply human; more than that, they all had one thing in common: they all loved the Park City. So thanks for getting us started, Isaac Sherman Jr.

INTRODUCTION

Is Bridgeport more corrupt than any other American city? Absolutely not. But a town that became a city for the main purpose of lining the pockets of its citizenry is certainly going to be susceptible to a bit of corruption. And that is what happened in Bridgeport, Connecticut, in 1836, and as the legendary baseball manager Casey Stengel once said, "You could look it up."

After 1836, Bridgeport moved on to rolling and rollicking times, and a great deal of it had to do with political leadership, a political leadership that through these many years has proven to be quite colorful, to say the least. To say the most, the term "felonious" seems to fit best.

The Park City has indeed had its share of rogues and renegades throughout the years, but to say it has been a complete feeding frenzy at the public trough would not be true. There have been numerous adept and honest political leaders in Bridgeport, and their legacies are just as vital as those of some of their more notorious colleagues.

Bridgeport is a city that lives, eats and breathes politics. In the diners and the pubs and the barbershops, politics is often the topic of the day. Residents in Bridgeport like to gripe long and loud about their municipal government. They may not always vote, but they like to complain.

The simple fact remains that Bridgeport itself is the largest employer within city limits, making political participation paramount for all those whose paychecks bear the city of Bridgeport logo. This is a simple matter of self-preservation. If you would like to keep your job, it might be wise to support the party in power at the ballot box. And for the last twenty-two years, that party has been the Democrats.

There is a certain amount of fear that exists in Bridgeport politics that has to do with people losing their jobs or having their livelihoods crippled through political retribution. I was astounded when a former director of communications for the city refused to be interviewed for this book although that person has not worked for the city in over six years. I was not astounded because they refused to be interviewed but because of the way their eyes widened in abject terror when I broached the subject. Others who demonstrated fear in terms of this project were a one-term Bridgeport city councilman who hasn't sought office in years and a prominent downtown business owner. I can certainly sympathize with all three people, but I wish that culture of fear did not exist in Bridgeport.

These were the exceptions, however. I was blessed with a positive response from the community and basically had some great conversations about this project during the months I worked on it.

One of the questions I had to ask myself was whether or not there is a real stigma attached to Bridgeport's political history, and I have come to the conclusion that there is. However, there is much more than just a stigma. There are heroes, role models, crooks, visionaries and more comic relief than one can imagine.

What exists here is the magic of politics, the feeling that something is real. Maybe I'm being a bit parochial, but I firmly believe that Park City residents are well aware that a vote for your local councilman is far more important than a vote for who will next reside at 1600 Pennsylvania Avenue. What's more important? Whether or not your obnoxious next-door neighbor can build a deck that protrudes onto your property or whether or not J.P. Morgan Chase is going to be sanctioned for antitrust violations?

Bridgeport residents know what counts. That is why they care. That is why more than a few of them rise and vocally assert their displeasure to members of the city council, the board of education and the mayor himself. Of course, their complaints probably will be summarily dismissed, but at least they have voiced their displeasure.

And we cannot discount the passion of those who are employed in government service. There are few scenes more vitriolic than Bridgeport decision makers who have been questioned about their findings or their veracity. Their reaction, I believe, could be universally described as "violently pissed off."

So what we have here in the Park City is passion—a passion for politics, a passion for history, a passion for a way of life, a passion for neighborhoods and a passion for the city. There is no shortage of characters who carry out that passion, and hopefully I can introduce you to some of them in this book.

Among them are our current mayor Bill Finch, who once led me out on the twelfth floor of 10 Middle Street, one of Bridgeport's few skyscrapers, in search of peregrine falcons; former mayor John Fabrizi, who once drove me in the dead of night to one of Bridgeport's most notorious housing projects to prove he wasn't afraid of anything; and P.T. Barnum himself, who, although he seems to enjoy a peaceful resting place in the bucolic environment of Mountain Grove Cemetery, somehow still seems to command control of Bridgeport.

I guess it was walking through Mountain Grove that first gave me the idea to write about this topic. I remembered reading *Ragtime* by the great American writer E.L. Doctorow and enjoying with pure glee how he described the graves of Barnum and his protégé, Charles Stratton, also known as General Tom Thumb. Doctorow also wrote of Lavinia Warren, the general's wife, and why she continued to live in the Park City after his death. The author wrote, "She lived in Bridgeport to be next to the grave of her husband, who had died many years before and was commemorated in stone atop a monumental column in Mountain Grove Cemetery."

As I looked up at the Stratton monument, perhaps the highest in the cemetery, and saw the great man's bust above a giant marble pillar, I thought, there he is: just a tiny man physically, but as he beckons eternity, he is larger than anyone. And that, my friends, is how I feel about the city of Bridgeport.

Part I

SETTING THE STAGE

1
ISAAC AND P.T.

I Daniel Sterling, warden of the Borough of Bridgeport do hereby forever adjourn this borough meeting, September 30, 1836.
Daniel Sterling

In the spring of 1836, the leading citizens of the town of Bridgeport were not happy. In fact, many were downright angry. The good citizens felt that they were mired under the borough system of government, and for the last several years, they had deemed this form of government wholly unsatisfactory.

Originally known as Stratfield, the village of Newfield was recognized by the young state's General Assembly in 1798. However, like Stratfield before it, Newfield remained a village of the town of Stratford. In 1800, the General Assembly stepped in again and made the village of Newfield a section of the borough of Bridgeport. This gave the newly created borough some semblance of independence from Stratford, but not totally. As Connecticut's first borough, Bridgeport received many of the benefits of a town but was not given any representation in the General Assembly. Those borough residents who were eligible to vote had to trek east across the Yellow Mill River into Stratford proper to cast their ballots.

The new configuration seemed to be well received by the residents of the borough, as prosperity was the order of the day for the small community. Then, suddenly in one swift stroke, contentment turned into resentment.

In the first of what would be many battles between Stratford and Bridgeport during the next two hundred years or so, in 1821 Stratford gave

Bridgeport the bums rush, severing ties with its former village. Bridgeport was now its own town, and that did not sit well with residents, who felt they were given short shrift by their neighbors in Stratford by the way the towns were divided.

As it turned out, Stratford had seized most of the waterfront, which left residents of the town now called Bridgeport seething. After more than a decade of being unhappy with Bridgeport's incorporation as a town, the leading citizens of the growing community decided to incorporate as a city.

The original charter committee for this purpose was established on April 8, 1836. The committee members were Stephen Lounsbury, Samuel Simons, Smith Tweedy, Fitch Wheeler, William H. Noble, Joseph Thompson and Charles DeForest. The seven men drafted an appeal to the state General Assembly in Hartford with their petitions. It did not take long for the legislature to act on Bridgeport's request, approving the petition in May. The legislators assigned October 3, 1836, as the date for the official incorporation, and that same date is now celebrated as Bridgeport's official birthday.

The final borough hearing was held on September 30, 1836, at the conclusion of which Daniel Sterling dramatically declared, "I Daniel Sterling, warden of the Borough of Bridgeport do hereby forever adjourn this borough meeting, September 30, 1836."

The assemblage had chosen Isaac Sherman Jr., a successful businessman, as Bridgeport's first mayor, and Sherman took office on October 3. Sherman owned a saddlery business with his brother Levi, and the two men also had an operation in Columbia, South Carolina.

The desire to become a city was not simply altruistic in terms of what form of government would be best for Bridgeport citizens. The move was about money and commerce, in particular bringing a railroad to the Park City. There was no rail service in Bridgeport, and the iron horse was quickly becoming the wonder of the nineteenth century. Railroads were also proving to be indispensable to cities that wanted to prosper.

Coincidentally or not, at the same time the Connecticut General Assembly was approving Bridgeport's request to be incorporated as a city, the Housatonic Railroad was also being chartered. Originally called Ousatonic Railroad by the locals, the company was chartered in 1836.

In March 1837, the new city received the borrowing power to loan money to the fledging railroad, and the wheels were in motion. Isaac Sherman had completed a historical transaction in just five months in office. The railroad would run from Bridgeport along the Housatonic River north to the Massachusetts

The arrival of the Housatonic Railroad in 1836 coincided with Bridgeport's incorporation as a city. The Housatonic ushered in the Park City's industrial age and helped make Bridgeport one of the major manufacturing centers in the Northeast. *Courtesy of the Bridgeport History Center, Bridgeport Public Library.*

border. In less than four years, on February 19, 1840, the Bridgeport to New Milford line was open for business, and on December 1, 1842, the route from Bridgeport to the Massachusetts state line also began operation.

Although the city of Bridgeport was established mainly because of greed and the opportunity for tremendous financial gain, the idea was an excellent one. Bringing the Housatonic Railroad to Bridgeport gave a kick start to Bridgeport's fledgling industrial base and, coupled with the Park City 's busy port system, soon turned the small community into a hub of industry. Alfred Bishop, a transplanted New Jersey farmer, was the president of the Housatonic Railroad and oversaw its completion. He is largely credited with being the individual most responsible for spurring Bridgeport's industrial growth.

As for Isaac Sherman, he served one year as mayor and then returned to the saddlery. He last held office in Bridgeport in 1841, when he served as the city's postmaster. He then uprooted his wife and three children to Batavia, New York, but his eyes soon turned west.

Sherman opened a branch of the saddlery in Saint Louis, and business was brisk. Unfortunately for Sherman, who had left his family behind in Batavia, westward expansion would prove fatal. There was a cholera outbreak in the

Gateway to the West in 1848, and Sherman tried to flee home to New York. He did not make it.

Sherman got as far as Freeport, Illinois, before succumbing to the dreaded disease on May 22, 1849, at the age of forty-eight. A report in the *Freeport Journal* described Sherman as a businessman from Bridgeport, Connecticut, whose friends and family would be gratified to know that every effort was made to save him. As for his family, the *Journal* reporter wrote they "will be called upon to mourn his mournful death."

There is some question as to where Bridgeport's first mayor was finally laid to rest. In those years, it was rare to transport a body for burial, so he may be buried in Freeport. There is also a chance that he was returned to Saint Louis because of cholera's nature as a communicable disease.

There is a plaque at Plot 17 in Mountain Grove Cemetery in Bridgeport for Sherman, but he is generally not believed to be buried there. The plaque reads:

In memory of Isaac Sherman Jr.

Who dies of cholera
May 22, 1849
Aged 48 yrs. And 7 mos.
Twas God's will in his own time
To take this mortal in his prime
Erected by his mother
Also of Levi Sherman
Who dies in St. Louis, Mo.
Jan. 13, 1852
Aged 48 yrs. And 9 mos.
Their souls went to God when he went Amen and
Their bodies are at rest in a far and distant land

The final two lines indicate that Levi stayed in Saint Louis to keep the saddlery in operation, but he, too, died in the West. The two community-spirited Bridgeport brothers are not here, but they certainly are remembered here.

SETTING THE STAGE

INTERLUDE

Honest Abe comes to town

Through the years, Bridgeport has been no stranger to political heavyweights coming to town to expound their philosophies. The town of Bridgeport received Revolutionary War hero Marquis de Lafayette warmly on a visit to America in 1824, and more recently the Park City welcomed President Barack Obama when he visited Bridgeport in 2010 to campaign for local Democrats, especially U.S. senatorial candidate Richard Blumenthal, who won his election handily.

Other political luminaries who have stopped by Bridgeport include George W. Bush, John F. Kennedy, Dwight D. Eisenhower, Franklin Delano Roosevelt and Dr. Martin Luther King Jr, to name a few. There are many more political heavyweights and presidents who have swung through the Park City, but the most notable has to be Abraham Lincoln, who spoke here on March 10, 1860, as he was wrapping up a campaign swing through New England.

Lincoln was in the midst of what was perhaps the most critical presidential campaign in American history. The Southern states had made well known their intention of seceding from the Union if Lincoln was elected president. The other candidates in the race were John C. Breckenridge of Kentucky of the Southern Democratic Party, who was favored by most Southern voters; John Bell of Tennessee of the Constitutional Union Party; and Lincoln's old foe Stephen A. Douglas, who had defeated Lincoln in the 1858 Illinois senatorial election amid the famed Lincoln-Douglas debates.

That night, Lincoln, the Republican nominee, was preaching to the converted. The audience was overwhelmingly pro-Union, antislavery and pro-Lincoln. The event was held at the newly built Washington Hall, and the crowd overflowed outside the building. Alas, there is no record of what Lincoln said on that historic occasion, but he was given a tremendous sendoff by the people of Bridgeport after heading out of the city and out of New England.

There is a plaque at McLevy Hall in downtown Bridgeport recognizing the historical importance of the event. It reads:

> *Abraham Lincoln visited this city Saturday evening March 10, 1860*
> *and delivered a political address before a large audience of citizens in*

Washington Hall, which was then a portion of this building. This tablet is placed here in commemoration of this event by the city of Bridgeport. MCMXI

Lincoln never returned to Bridgeport and the speech he gave at Washington Hall on March 10, 1860, was the last speech he ever gave in New England.

P.T. and Politics

P.T. Barnum was an avid Lincoln supporter, and he was there that Saturday night in March, vocally supporting the Republican candidate with gusto. The showman even kept his current mansion, Lindencroft, illuminated throughout the entire night in Lincoln's honor.

Barnum would show his exuberant support for the Union cause in a far more dramatic manner a little more than a year later. On August 24, 1861, Ellis B. Schnable, who Barnum called "a broken down politician from Pennsylvania," was scheduled to speak at a peace rally in Stepney, ten miles north of Bridgeport, which is now part of the town of Monroe. Schnable was well known as a rabid antiwar instigator and, according to the *Hartford Post*, was thrown in jail five days later for rabble rousing in the Litchfield County village of Morris.

Barnum and a few of his buddies, including Elias Howe, the inventor of the sewing machine who would later serve as a private in the Union army, traveled north to see what was happening in Stepney. They were joined there by dozens of soldiers at home on furlough. Barnum quickly co-opted the meeting and turned it into a pro-Union rally.

The *Bridgeport Daily Advertiser and Weekly Farmer* was a Copperhead newspaper. Northerners who supported the Southern cause in the Civil War were known as Copperheads, and there were fewer vile epithets that could be hurled in a pro-Union state such as Connecticut. Unfortunately for the newspaper, many participants of the Stepney rally were so fired up that they marched into Bridgeport and destroyed the newspaper's office. Barnum was gleeful and wrote to President Lincoln of the developments. As Barnum's biographer A.H. Saxon points out, "There were no more peace meetings in Connecticut." For obvious reasons, Barnum probably thought.

Lincoln and the Civil War inspired Barnum to enter politics at the end of the war, and he was elected to two terms in the state legislature. He then

The P.T. Barnum Museum in downtown Bridgeport. Barnum is the only mayor of Bridgeport with his own museum, and his iconic shadow still towers over the city. *Courtesy of Gerri Whitlock.*

turned his eyes to the national scene and ran for Congress in 1867, but he lost the election to William H. Barnum of Salisbury, a distant cousin.

Barnum returned to politics in 1875 at the behest of his fellow Republicans who wanted him to run for mayor of the Park City, a fitting title since Barnum had donated one of Bridgeport's crown jewels, the Frederick Law

Olmstead–designed Seaside Park. The master showman would also go on to found Bridgeport Hospital and many other local institutions. During the mayoral campaign, Barnum also received widespread Democratic support and had little trouble trouncing his Democratic opponent, Frederick Hurd.

Barnum was an extremely proactive mayor and scandal free, but he was controversial. He was hearing criticism from a time when he was instrumental in a land deal that closed the Stratfield Cemetery on the west side of Park Avenue, near what are now Cottage and Hanover Streets. That area of the city was being rapidly developed, and Mountain Grove Cemetery, which had Barnum's financial backing, was open and had lots of room.

However, the remains of more than three thousand residents of Stratfield Cemetery had to be moved to Mountain Grove, and that is where the situation got somewhat messy. Barnum was accused of disinterring the remains in a slipshod manner. He had brokered a deal with David W. Sherwood, a former butcher, to do the work, and some claim that the bones of loved ones were being strewn across city streets as they fell out of decaying coffins to the cobblestones below.

These charges were vigorously denied by Barnum and dismissed as a tempest in a teapot, but the story persists to this day. In fact, there are still some Bridgeport residents who do not like to walk down Cottage Street. The political controversy faded, but the new mayor was often tweaked by his enemies at the *Bridgeport Daily Advertiser and Weekly Farmer* who certainly still remembered the Civil War destruction of their newspaper offices.

Another problem Barnum faced was that Bridgeport was now a Democratic city and the common council was composed of nearly all Democrats. The Democrats were opposed to many of Barnum's initiatives, and this frustrated the old showman.

Yet he was able to accomplish a great deal during his one year in office. A national temperance leader, Barnum vigorously enforced the laws that would not allow saloons to open on Sundays, competitively awarded the gas contracts for the city's street lamps and demanded an improved water supply from the Bridgeport Hydraulic Company. In fact, Barnum demanded the company be sold to the city if it could not get its act together.

At the end of his term he wrote, "My ambition is to be a poor politician. The Mayor and the Common Council have no right to be influenced by political or personal feelings. Our business is to manage the affairs of the city justly, economically and for the greatest good of the entire community."

Barnum was also chums with author Samuel Clemens, also known as Mark Twain. The legendary writer paid many visits to the circus

Iranistan, P.T. Barnum's first and most opulent mansion, burned to the ground in December 1857. In his autobiography, he wrote, "My beautiful Iranistan is gone!" *Drawing courtesy of the Bridgeport History Center, Bridgeport Public Library.*

impresario at his various mansions throughout the years, and those trips perhaps may have been responsible for the following passage in the classic novel *A Connecticut Yankee in King Arthur's Court*:

> *We saw a far away town sleeping in a valley by a winding river; and beyond it on a hill, a vast gray fortress, with towers and turrets, the first I had ever seen out of a picture.*
> *"Bridgeport," said I, pointing.*
> *"Camelot," said he.*

After his stint as mayor, Barnum served two more terms in the state General Assembly as a Bridgeport representative, and that was the last elected office he held until his death on April 7, 1891. He was interred at his beloved Mountain Grove and departed as the most famous man in the world at the time and a Bridgeport legend for all time.

2

POLITICAL POWER TAKES SHAPE

You have a record that cannot be duplicated by any city in this country.
Franklin Delano Roosevelt

Barnum had departed from the scene, the twentieth century beckoned and Bridgeport was more and more becoming one of the most important industrial centers in the Northeast. Such a situation meant there was money to be made and politics to be practiced.

Companies such as the Howe Sewing Machine Company, Frisbie's Pies, Bridgeport Brass, the Bryant Electric Company and Reads Department Store were attracting workers and entrepreneurs to the city. The quality of life was high, as the city had carried out a parks plan some years earlier.

As Bridgeport became thoroughly industrialized, smog choked the city, vision was limited and foul odors permeated the streets. P.T. Barnum had donated beautiful Seaside Park to the city, featuring miles of oceanfront beach on Long Island Sound. The park was designed by Frederick Law Olmstead, who, among other landscape masterpieces, had created Central Park in New York City and the Emerald Necklace in Boston.

With more residents arriving due to the rapid business growth, the population toward the northern borders of the Park City began to grow. For those Bridgeporters living in the North End, there were acres of parkland to be found at Beardsley Park, where denizens could escape the industrial vibe of the city and relax in the beauty of nature.

SETTING THE STAGE

Beardsley Park is aptly named, for it exists because of the beneficence of one man, James Beardsley. The park's namesake was a Bridgeport businessman, public servant and philanthropist. In the last years of his life, Beardsley bequeathed what amounted to nearly sixty acres of his private holdings to the city, with the caveat that the land be turned into a public park.

James Beardsley has gone down as one of the most important men in Bridgeport history, yet he came to a tragic end. The seventy-two-year-old bachelor lived quietly in Bridgeport with his elderly spinster sister. The wealthy Beardsley siblings were tempting targets for highwaymen, and robbers invaded the Beardsley home on December 20, 1892. Beardsley suffered a stomach wound during the attack and soon developed peritonitis. The philanthropist lived through Christmas but died on New Year's Day 1893.

In his honor, the people of Bridgeport erected a statue of Beardsley, sculpted by Charles Henry Niehaus and unveiled on June 21, 1909. Since that first day of summer more than a century ago, Mr. James Beardsley, one of the Park City's favorite sons, has smiled on the hundreds of thousands of revelers who descend on the park to picnic, frolic, enjoy nature and marvel that in Connecticut's busiest city such an emerald jewel is there for their enjoyment.

Yes, Bridgeport was changing in many ways. And Bridgeport politics were changing with the city. Working for the City of Bridgeport meant a guaranteed paycheck, and this guaranteed paycheck would be provided by the municipal government. As a result, employees needed to be loyal to the powers running the city, and that meant political patronage became a main staple of Bridgeport city government.

Gone were the days when an Isaac Sherman Jr. or a P.T. Barnum would agree to seek elective office for purely altruistic reasons. Politicians were still full of community spirit and were civic minded, but seeking office now also meant power, money and self-interest.

Bridgeport had evolved as a mostly Democratic city at the end of the nineteenth century, but the days of Republican ascendency were on the horizon. They would arrive in 1911 with the election of Republican mayor Clifford B. Wilson, giving the GOP effective control of Park City government for most of the next twenty years.

Wilson was opposed in the election by Democrat John M. Donnelly. Also in the race was Socialist Jasper McLevy, making his first run for the city's highest office in an attempt to replace Democratic incumbent Edward T. Buckingham.

McLevy's presence in the race was somewhat alarming to the leaders of Bridgeport's two major parties. According to a report in the November 1, 1911 edition of the *Bridgeport Evening Post*, "Astounding as it may seem there are now observing politicians who say that the contest on Election Day will be between the Republicans and the Socialists. It is impossible to say how this belief is warranted."

Wilson wound up winning the election, defeating Donnelly with a plurality of 279 votes. For a newcomer and running as a member of a political party perceived as being somewhat radical, McLevy made a strong showing, polling 3,623 votes, about 2,000 behind Wilson. Jasper McLevy would be heard from again.

The cigar-smoking Wilson was a coroner by trade, and he presided over what was perhaps the most prosperous era in Bridgeport history. This was the age of World War I, when the Park City earned another nickname, the "Arsenal of Democracy," a moniker earned as Bridgeport took the lead as the most important arms manufacturer in the world.

Wilson was considered a progressive Republican in the Theodore Roosevelt mode, and he patterned his style of governing as that of a chief executive of a company. He was elected for five terms. However, his progressive style of governing would never have been put in place if not for the power behind the throne: Republican boss John T. King.

King well understood the spoils system and became Bridgeport's king of patronage. He established a system that ensured both Republicans and Democrats received the spoils of Bridgeport's political system and had jobs. Of course, this meant that members of both parties supported Wilson, effectively neutering any Democratic candidate's chance to unseat the popular mayor.

Wilson has gone down in Bridgeport history as one of the city's most effective mayors. He commissioned the first city plan, and the results included new playgrounds, recreational programs, old-age hospitals and health clinics. Wilson was also extremely popular with women as he was an early and ardent supporter of women's suffrage.

When World War I arrived during his term, Bridgeport industry was ready from the war's outbreak in 1914. Companies such as Remington Arms and the Lake Torpedo Boat Company were supplying the British, French and Russians with most of their weaponry. When the United States entered the war in April 1917, the Arsenal of Democracy was responsible for more than two-thirds of the munitions in use by the Allies.

Perhaps the most astounding of these arms factories was Remington Arms on the East Side of Bridgeport. The plant was established in 1867 and originally incorporated as the Union Metallic Cartridge Company, noted for its development of metallic cartridges. Union Metallic Cartridge merged with the Remington Arms Corporation to form Remington Arms.

The Remington munitions plant developed the first paper shot shells successfully manufactured in the United States and became the first company to produce and make several other munitions advancements. A unique component of the plant was the approximately 130-foot-tall shot tower, which is now one of the few remaining shot towers in the entire country.

Although the war was an absolute tragedy and would change the face of history forever, it was a time of unbridled prosperity for the city of Bridgeport. The Park City's population increased from 100,000 to 150,000 during Wilson's tenure, and Remington Arms alone was hiring 1,400 to 1,600 new employees per month.

INTERLUDE

FDR Praises the Arsenal of Democracy

On May 20, 1917, the young assistant secretary of the navy, Franklin Delano Roosevelt, arrived in Bridgeport for a whirlwind tour of the Arsenal of Democracy. The assistant secretary was accompanied by Mayor Clifford B. Wilson and given a hero's welcome wherever he went.

Roosevelt visited Remington Arms, the Lake Torpedo Boat Company and the Locomobile Company of America, whose factory had converted from making luxury cars to making army trucks. FDR also attended a luncheon, dinner and a Red Cross ballroom dance before departing on a late train to return to Washington, D.C.

During a stop at the American and British Company, Roosevelt told an enthusiastic crowd estimated at more than four thousand by the *Bridgeport Evening Post* that "you have a record that cannot be duplicated by any city in the country."

Shortly afterward, Roosevelt gave the throng more music for its ears, taking on the despised Kaiser Wilhelm II of Germany. "Don't let the Kaiser die as Wilhelm the II," Roosevelt bellowed to the crowd. "Let's make him Wilhelm the Last."

Roosevelt was a state senator from Westchester County in New York when he chose to enthusiastically support New Jersey's progressive governor

Assistant Secretary of the Navy Franklin Delano Roosevelt, accompanied by Bridgeport mayor Clifford B. Wilson, addresses more than four thousand workers at the American and British Company in May 1917. *Courtesy of the Bridgeport History Center, Bridgeport Public Library.*

Woodrow Wilson in his candidacy for president of the United States in 1912. Wilson made note of the New Yorker's support and sought to find a place for Roosevelt in his new administration.

When Secretary of the Navy Josephus Daniels tapped him to be his assistant, FDR jumped at the opportunity. By all accounts, Roosevelt loved his job as assistant secretary, not only because of the ceremonial aspect of the position that he so enjoyed but also because he helped to shape naval policy, especially after the United States entered the war in April 1917.

He served as assistant secretary of the navy from 1913 to 1920, when he was chosen by the Democrats as the vice presidential nominee and became the running mate of James Middleton Cox in the 1920 election. Senator Warren G. Harding, a former newspaper editor from Ohio, soundly trounced Cox. In a few years, Harding would posthumously play a role in Bridgeport history, and the man known as FDR would return triumphantly to the national stage.

THE BRIDGE SCANDALS

Wilson's ten-year run as mayor came to an end in 1921, when he was voted out of office in favor of Democrat Fred Atwater. The Democratic ascendency didn't last long, and the Republicans were back in power in 1923, when King engineered the election of F.W. Behrens, a local butcher.

Mrs. Florence Harding came to Bridgeport in 1924 to dedicate Warren Harding High School on the East Side. President Harding died suddenly in 1923. *Courtesy of the Bridgeport History Center, Bridgeport Public Library.*

During Behrens's term in 1924, a new high school was built in the city and was named for the late president Warren G. Harding. Harding had died suddenly in 1923, elevating former Massachusetts governor Calvin Coolidge to the presidency. Mrs. Florence Harding was on hand for the dedication ceremony as Harding High School became the first public building in the country to be named for Warren Harding.

It's ironic that Harding High School was named after the late president as he is now almost universally regarded as the worst president in the history of the United States. A former newspaperman, Harding eventually became a U.S. senator. He was a notorious womanizer, and although he was personally honest, many members of his administration became caught up in the Teapot Dome scandal, a scheme involving the nation's oil reserves that was generally considered the worst presidential scandal in American history until Watergate during the Nixon years.

King, who was also tainted by the Teapot Dome scandal but never charged, died in 1926, leaving Behrens on his own. Behrens would serve three terms but eventually was done in by his own local scandal.

The Yellow Mill Bridge on the East Side of the city had recently been completed and was generally considered an architectural marvel. Perhaps that was why the ultimate cost of the bridge was so high. Or perhaps it was graft. In the end, naturally, it turned out to be graft.

An investigation uncovered that the cost overrun for the city was nearly $140,000. This was due to corruption on the part of the Bridge Commission, not Behrens. The construction company selected by the commission to build the bridge set up a dummy corporation, through which materials to build the bridge were purchased. Members of the bridge commission profited from the move, and the city was left holding the bag.

This came on the heels of the so-called Ripper Bill, a bill passed by the state legislature that gave control of the city's finances to the state. This occurred because the state tax commissioner discovered that Bridgeport had more than $3 million in uncollected tax bills outstanding.

These developments finished Behrens and the Republicans. No member of the Grand Old Party would be elected mayor of Bridgeport until Nicholas Panuzio in 1971. The Democrats resurrected Edward T. Buckingham, and he won the 1929 election to replace Behrens.

Behrens returned to being a butcher and opened up a meat market in the city. Retired from politics, he became famous around the Park City for hosting massive dinners for his old political cronies and friends, whom he called the "Irish Parliament."

Bridgeport Socialists were poised to assume political power thanks to the Great Depression and the leadership of Jasper McLevy. *Courtesy of the Bridgeport History Center, Bridgeport Public Library.*

Buckingham soon had his own problems. Shortly after his election, a crisis involving repairs to the Stratford Avenue Bridge arose. The repairs to the bridge were originally estimated to cost approximately $33,000. The final bill came in at a figure closer to $280,000. Buckingham blamed the engineering company but this $250,000 "mistake" aroused the ire of Bridgeporters who had had their fill of bridge troubles.

During these years of woe, Jasper McLevy had stuck around, a Socialist thorn in the side of both the Republicans and the Democrats. A constant office seeker and sidewalk politician, he had run for nearly every office imaginable and had slowly gained statewide respect. In the 1931 election, Buckingham managed to get reelected, but McLevy had leapfrogged the Republican candidate and finished second behind the incumbent by less than three thousand votes. The Socialists were on the move.

In the end, it was the Great Depression that finished Buckingham and the Democrats. Bridgeport's mayor was in a similar position to President Herbert

Hoover. He was the head guy, and he was going to take the blame no matter what happened. People were miserable and in dire economic straits, and they believed a change had to take place. Plus, it did not help Buckingham that he was driven in a chauffeured limousine accompanied by a police escort wherever he went. People were angry and upset at Buckingham's flaunting of his power and prestige, and that mood change helped set the stage for the Bridgeport mayoral election of 1933.

3

JASPER

Let the guy who put it there take it away.
Pete Brewster

Buckingham managed to escape the humiliation he undoubtedly knew was coming. He declined to run for reelection and went to work for the State of Connecticut. The new Democratic candidate was a fellow named James L. Dunn, who was soundly beaten. Jasper McLevy and the Socialists were now in power. The Republicans were not a factor in the election. More than 83 percent of registered voters turned out to vote in the election, and McLevy finished with 48 percent of the vote with more than twenty-two thousand ballots cast in his favor.

The new mayor's victory received not only statewide but also national attention. "It was the talk of the town up here. Nobody could believe it, but we were all cheering for Jasper McLevy," recalled John D. Sullivan, a union leader for the United Steelworkers of America from Worcester, Massachusetts. "It was magnificent." This revelation is not all that surprising as Worcester, a manufacturing town on the shores of Lake Quinsigamond about forty-five miles west of Boston in Central Massachusetts, was a city very much like Bridgeport.

The local Communist Party leader told the *Bridgeport Times-Star*, "It wasn't a protest vote, it was more than that. This proved that there was this process of becoming radicalized and they turned to McLevy. They thought he was a Socialist."

In actuality, McLevy's message was mostly economics in government, and his penuriousness became legendary in Bridgeport lore. But his thrift is the major reason he detested the spoils system that had dominated Bridgeport politics since the turn of the century. A roofer by trade, McLevy's secret to success was relatively simple: stay power. A stubborn Bridgeporter of Scottish stock, McLevy never stopped hammering home his message since he first ran for office in 1903. McLevy's message was not the traditional socialist message, although he strongly believed that the workingman should have as fair a shot in life as the rich man. McLevy was also a vigorous union man, and this proved to be one of the major reasons he was boosted into office in 1933.

Perhaps the best description of the Bridgeport mayor was made by Harold J. Bingham, who wrote that he was "more McLevy than Socialist, more Republican than Democrat, and more for Bridgeport than any."

After ridding the city of Buckingham's limo and saving Bridgeport taxpayers that unnecessary expense, one of McLevy's early moves was instituting the civil service system, whereby city employees were hired by test results and not by whom they supported politically. This effectively destroyed the patronage system that had been the lifeblood of Park City politics for years.

As Bridgeport journalist Lennie Grimaldi aptly points out in his seminal work *Only in Bridgeport*, this move had a dual effect. Not only did civil service reform remove the spoils system the mayor could not stand, but it also augmented McLevy's political base. He now had hundreds of city workers who would be forever loyal to him because they now had something they had never had before: job protection. No longer did they have to worry about still having a job if their candidate lost on election day.

The citizenry's disaffection with the Democrats and Republicans did not automatically dictate that Jasper McLevy was out of the woods politically. McLevy had generally earned plaudits for his first term, but that did not necessarily mean that the two major parties were ready to concede the mayoral office to the Socialist party on a permanent basis. As a result, the Republicans pulled out the big guns—or in this case, the big gun. Clifford B. Wilson, arguably Bridgeport's most popular mayor, save for P.T. Barnum, stepped out of retirement and into the spotlight to challenge McLevy.

Wilson was popular not only in Bridgeport but also throughout the state. The Park City mayor was also Connecticut's lieutenant governor from 1915 through 1921, holding both offices at the same time. In fact, he had been considered gubernatorial material until losing the mayoral chair to Fred Atwater in 1921.

In the end, all those positives that Wilson brought to the table proved not to be enough to dethrone McLevy. The residents still held a great deal of animosity toward the major parties stemming from the earlier scandals, and most felt McLevy had done a decent job—why throw him out of office? McLevy wouldn't face another serious challenge for twenty years.

As for Wilson, 1935 proved to be his last hurrah in politics. The five-time Park City mayor died of a heart attack in nearby Weston in 1943. He was sixty-three years old.

Jasper McLevy was fifty-five years old when he was finally elected mayor in 1933. He had begun campaigning for various offices in 1903 when he

McLevy finished up a roofing job on his first day in office. When he was ousted twenty-four years later, McLevy quipped, "I can always go back to roofing." *Courtesy of the Bridgeport History Center, Bridgeport Public Library.*

was twenty-five. Perhaps it was his hardy ancestry rooted in the highlands of Scotland or simply sheer determination, but Bridgeporters certainly admired his thirty-years of determination. Eventually, the citizenry came to like his ideas.

He was nothing if not pragmatic. For example, McLevy was a roofer by trade, and during his mayoral tenure, he insisted that every new building constructed by the City of Bridgeport have a slate roof, putting his years of experience in the roofing business to work for the city. Park City residents admired that type of practicality.

There is no doubt that McLevy's most lasting legacy was his thriftiness. Going back to the Behrens administration and continuing with Buckingham's, McLevy was appalled at the amount of bonded debt that the city was racking up and issued warnings about this debt in all of his campaigns. Now that he was in power, the new mayor intended to do something about it.

Within a few years in office, McLevy had balanced Bridgeport's books and held the line on city taxes. The main way the mayor had tackled the problem was by reducing expenditures. He also changed city policies that he thought were wasteful. For example, McLevy thought that the city was throwing away too much money on its contract with trash collectors and private incinerators, so he simply purchased an incinerator and brought that particular city service in house.

The mayor's frugality did not stop with city money. It also extended to his own personal finances. He had a daily cup of tea at Van Dyke's Restaurant, which was then located at 915 Main Street, and never failed to leave the waitress a ten-cent tip.

Charlie Coviello, a Park City politician who would later run for mayor several times himself, was McLevy's paperboy as a youth.

"How do you remember Jasper McLevy?" Coviello was asked.

"Cheap," he replied.

Easily the most famous of the McLevy stories about his thriftiness is his legendary reluctance to plow the city's streets. There was a lot of griping about this by residents and in the newspapers, and McLevy allegedly said, "God put the snow there, let God take it away."

As most Bridgeport residents know, Jasper McLevy never muttered those words, but he has always received the credit for one of the most famous phrases associated with the Park City.

In reality, Pete Brewster, Bridgeport's director of Public Works, was sitting in a local bar having a few beers with the regulars one night in the winter of 1938. The joint was also a hangout for a lot of local newspapermen who began ribbing Brewster about the city's slow response to clearing Bridgeport

Some Bridgeporters blamed McLevy's penuriousness for the condition of the city's streets during the blizzard of 1938. *Courtesy of the Bridgeport History Center, Bridgeport Public Library.*

streets. After all, Bridgeport is in New England; the city has to expect some snow, argued the members of the fourth estate.

Finally fed up with the heckling, Brewster snapped, "Let the guy who put it there take it away." But it went down in history as Jasper McLevy's most famous quip.

McLevy enjoys a light moment with Governors Wilbur Cross (center) and Raymond Baldwin (right). The three had just finished the rollicking 1938 gubernatorial campaign in which McLevy's presence helped Baldwin unseat Cross. *Courtesy of the Bridgeport History Center, Bridgeport Public Library.*

McLevy remained a force in state politics throughout his tenure. Here he is pictured with then congressman Abraham Ribbicoff (left) and Senator William Benton (center). *Courtesy of the Bridgeport History Center, Bridgeport Public Library.*

McLevy tried to capitalize on his growing statewide reputation by running for governor in 1938. At the time, it seemed next to impossible for a Socialist to be elected governor of Connecticut, but McLevy's reputation for frugality and honest government netted him a miraculous 166,000 votes. Needless to say, McLevy carried Bridgeport.

McLevy's total was enough to knock four-term Democratic incumbent Wilbur Cross out of office. Cross was an old political enemy, and McLevy felt no qualms about seeing the incumbent's reelection bid bite the dust. Republican Raymond Baldwin won the election by a scant 2,688 votes, and there is little question that the Bridgeport mayor made the difference.

Although McLevy failed in his bid for state office, he had no such worries back home in the Park City. For years, McLevy had almost no competition in Bridgeport. He worked well with the leadership of both the Democrats and the Republicans—Cornelius Mulvihill and Edward Sandula, respectively—and still had the strong union base and tremendous support from city employees. Consequently, he was virtually unbeatable.

The mayor cutting his birthday cake as wife Vida and dog Lassie look on. *Courtesy of the Bridgeport History Center, Bridgeport Public Library.*

As a result, McLevy defeated a string of political nonentities who lined up like bowling pins against him. For more than two decades, the Socialist McLevy controlled Park City politics. He could have ruled with an iron fist, but he didn't. That was another reason McLevy was so popular with the average Bridgeport resident. He was accessible and he was one of them.

With the dawn of the 1950s, McLevy's popularity began to wane slightly. This was not entirely perceptible, as he was still winning elections. The margins of victory were getting smaller and smaller, however.

In 1955, McLevy received a strong challenge from a young Democrat, a lawyer named Samuel Tedesco, whose campaign was managed by Cornelius

Jasper McLevy's widow, Vida, and Mayor Hugh Curran observe the late mayor's newly unveiled portrait at city hall. *Courtesy of the Bridgeport History Center, Bridgeport Public Library.*

Mulvihill. In that race, McLevy prevailed by only 5,300 votes, a far cry from the landslides of yesteryear.

In the end, what doomed McLevy was the thriftiness he championed and that had once made him so tremendously popular. The Park City was woefully underdeveloped, and Bridgeport businessmen were tired of the mayor's refusal to spend money. Their traditional support was rapidly waning.

McLevy's penny-pinching ways proved a superb panacea in their day, but eventually, this thriftiness came back to haunt Bridgeport. With almost no development during McLevy's unprecedented twenty-four-year reign, the Park City was rife for development and, therefore, rife for corruption.

Tedesco challenged the incumbent mayor again in 1957, and the race went down to the wire. In a rally at the Holy Trinity Slovak Club on the Sunday before the election, Tedesco told his supporters, "It is an American privilege to vote."

The city responded with a near record turnout of 53,779 voters. When the smoke cleared, Tedesco had tallied 24,386 votes to the incumbent's 24,225, a difference of a mere 161 votes. Showing the complete irrelevance of the Bridgeport Republican party in 1957, the GOP candidate, Domenick Cocco, had 5,168 ballots cast on his behalf. In any event, the seventy-nine-year old McLevy was through as Bridgeport's mayor.

"Now I'll have to find something else to do," he quipped.

But McLevy was not through with politics. He ran for governor in 1958, mayor in 1959 and congressman in 1960. He was unsuccessful in all three comeback attempts before a stroke forced his retirement from politics. Jasper McLevy died on November 20, 1962, at the age of eighty-four.

Part II

MISCHIEF TIME

4
AN ERA ENDS AND THE
GILDED AGE BEGINS

We have met the enemy and he is us.
Pogo Possum

In the early morning hours of November 6, 1957, Barnum School on Waterview Avenue on the East Side of Bridgeport was dark and quiet. Suddenly, someone stealthily crept into the building, disturbing the silence.

What was he after? The intruder was apparently after the voting machines that would be used that day in the hotly contested Bridgeport mayoral election between twenty-four-year Socialist incumbent Jasper McLevy and upstart Democratic challenger Samuel Tedesco.

The intruder knew what he was doing as he successfully tampered with the machine. He figured two hundred votes for Tedesco would do the job. The intruder tinkered with the machine and then slithered back out of the building, leaving Barnum School in silence once again, hours before the first actual vote was cast.

Fast-forward to later that night when the votes were counted. Tedesco was the winner of the election by a plurality of 161 votes. The 200 votes supplied by the stealthy Democratic operative had done the trick, and McLevy's twelve-term reign had ended.

Or so the story goes. McLevy supporters quickly floated that theory after the election, and although nothing has ever been proven, this story is widely accepted as fact. Most Bridgeporters today who were around back in 1957 still refer to the election that ended Jasper McLevy's twenty-four years in office as "disputed."

Interlude

Sam Tedesco welcomes JFK and MLK

If the tale is indeed true, the man behind the scheme was Cornelius "Connie" Mulvihill, the head of the Democratic Party and the man behind Tedesco. Mulvihill was the nephew of Denis Mulvihill, an Irish-born coal shoveler who became mayor of Bridgeport in 1901 and served until 1905. Denis Mulvihill welcomed President Theodore Roosevelt to Bridgeport in 1902, and Connie Mulvihill would enjoy a similar experience in 1960, when he and Mayor Tedesco welcomed presidential candidate John F. Kennedy to the Park City.

There is little question that Senator Kennedy had taken Connecticut by storm. More than thirty thousand people greeted the future president when he landed at Waterbury Airport at 3:00 a.m. in the morning, and by the time he reached the Bridgeport train station on Water Street at 1:00 p.m. on Sunday, November 6, an overflow crowd was waiting for him in the Park City as well. Police estimated a crowd of more than six thousand jammed into the small space. As he would time and again through the years, Kennedy thrilled the crowd with his oration and his attacks on his opponent, Vice President Richard M. Nixon.

"The choice for you is clear," JFK told his audience. "The choice is between those who look to the past and those who look to the future. This is an important election. The office of the Presidency is key. The Presidency is the most important office, not only in the United States, but in the free world, and I cannot believe that in 1960 we are going to select as President of the United States a man who is described by his close friend, Governor Rockefeller as a question mark. So on Tuesday, give us your help, your hand, your voice, your vote, and we will win."

Kennedy took Connecticut by more than ninety thousand votes.

One of the other main highlights of Tedesco's tenure in office was greeting another leader, an event that took place when Dr. Martin Luther King Jr. gave a speech at the Klein Memorial Auditorium in March 1961. More than 2,700 people heard Dr. King urge newly elected President Kennedy to strongly enforce civil rights laws.

The Door Is Open for Development

The election of 1957 was not the beginning of corruption in the Park City, as scandals had frequently been part of the Bridgeport political scene. Yet Tedesco's election did mark the beginning of unprecedented development in the Park City for both good and ill.

Tedesco did create a permanent black eye for himself early in his administration by demolishing the Harral-Wheeler House, the city's architectural gem. In 1956, ninety-one-year-old Arthur C. Wheeler died and bequeathed the house to the city, with his will expressly stating that the house could only be used for educational or park purposes. During his campaign, Tedesco said he wanted to use the house as a museum or for cultural purposes.

Essentially, he lied. While civic

Mayor Hugh Curran launched a new era of artistic development in the Park City. *Courtesy of the Bridgeport History Center, Bridgeport Public Library.*

groups, including the Bridgeport Historical Society, argued about the best use for the mansion, Tedesco had it torn down and replaced with a parking lot, in violation of Arthur C. Wheeler's will. This rogue action garnered national attention, all of it bad. Perhaps for the first, but certainly not the last time, Sam Tedesco had turned Bridgeport into the laughing stock of America.

Development took off under Tedesco, and he was responsible for completely changing the face of downtown, particularly on State Street. Bridgeport was long known for its thriving downtown, particularly on Thursday nights, when residents would roam Main Street for shopping and dining. Perhaps the changes brought by this new development sounded the death knell for the Park City's downtown, and in the not too distant future, the once thriving area would be barren, especially at night.

The project transformed downtown from a pedestrian paradise to an area encircled by highways, namely I-95 and Route 25, known locally as the Thruway and the Connector. The business community was hoping that the easy access would attract a bevy of new businesses downtown, but that was not the case.

"It was a disaster," said Robert T. Keeley Jr., who went on to become the longest-serving state legislator in city history. "It cut right through the heart of downtown and destroyed a lot of businesses. It wrecked downtown."

Still, there was an obvious need for urban renewal in Bridgeport. McLevy simply did not like to spend money, which was fine for the budget, but it left the city's infrastructure in dire need of repair. Schools were badly outmoded, and the physical appearance of the city as a whole had suffered.

Tedesco was certainly cheered on by the business community, which had grown quite tired of McLevy's miserliness and was champing at the bit for new development in the Park City. Businessmen cheered Tedesco on with the slogan "Brand New Bridgeport" and were avid supporters of the fifty-two-acre State Street redevelopment project.

With the business community behind him, Tedesco had invaluable allies not only on the development front but also on the political front. This was true despite the dominant presence of Edward Sandula, who had single-handedly

Longtime Republican boss Edward Sandula (center) was defeated in his 1959 mayoral race against Tedesco despite warm wishes from President Dwight D. Eisenhower. *Courtesy of the Bridgeport History Center, Bridgeport Public Library.*

controlled the Republican party for years. Tedesco enjoyed comfortable victories throughout his eight-year tenure, choosing not to run in 1965. His only electoral loss was his 1955 defeat at the hands of Jasper McLevy.

Still, there were those who were wary of too much growth and warned of its consequences. Looking back during a recent interview, a prominent Bridgeport developer told a reporter, "It all started with Tedesco. That's when it all started. I don't know if it was him, I doubt it. But that's when you couldn't just make a proposal any more. Suddenly you couldn't do anything here without greasing somebody's palm. That's when you knew you had to pay to play in Bridgeport."

The State Street redevelopment project required a great deal of demolition. Churches, fire houses, schools and parking garages were among many of the downtown structures that felt the cold steel of the wrecking ball that was first swung in September 1962. Demolishing buildings means demolition contracts, and the Bridgeport demolition industry has been historically rife with graft.

Looking back, it is hard to imagine that Sam Tedesco was crooked in any way, but the policies he instituted paved the way for shenanigans. Tedesco was a city judge when he was elected in 1957 and a Superior Court judge when he retired from public life. Tedesco also served as Connecticut's seventy-sixth lieutenant governor from 1963 to 1966 in the administration of Governor John Dempsey, joining Clifford B. Wilson as mayors of Bridgeport who simultaneously served in that state position. The former mayor died in 2003 at the age of eighty-eight.

Interlude

Pogo

From the 1940s through the 1970s, the most popular political comic strip in the country was Pogo, written by Bridgeport's own Walt Kelly, a 1930 graduate of the six-year-old Warren Harding High School and a reporter and cartoonist for the *Bridgeport Post*.

Kelly set his famed comic strip in Georgia in the Okefenokee Swamp, and Kelly's main characters were colorful animals. The Bridgeport native had his characters speak in swamp speak, and it was in that language that the swamp creatures wryly commented on the issues of the day.

Harding High grad Walt Kelly drawing his most famous character, Pogo Possum. *Courtesy of the Bridgeport History Center, Bridgeport Public Library.*

The lead character was Pogo Possum, who reluctantly campaigned for the presidency in both the 1952 and 1956 elections, although he lost to Dwight Eisenhower both times. Kelly caricatured infamous Senator Joe McCarthy's Communist witch hunts with a wildcat named Simple J. Malarkey. In 1960, Kelly's candidate was an egg with two protruding webbed feet, a commentary on candidate John F. Kennedy's youth. Kelly maintained that his election parodies were designed to get people out to vote and cautioned people not to vote for anyone on the extreme left, the extreme right or the extreme middle.

One of Pogo's recurring characters was P.T. Bridgeport, an homage to Kelly's hometown and its leading citizen. P.T. Bridgeport was a bear, a flamboyant impresario who, no surprise here, was also a circus operator. One of the Bridgeport native's most colorful characters, the bear wore a straw boater, spats, vest, an ascot complete with a stick pin and a fur-lined plaid overcoat.

An amiable blowhard and charlatan, P.T. Bridgeport's speech balloons resembled nineteenth-century circus posters, symbolizing his theatrical speech pattern and his carnival barker's sales spiel. P.T. Bridgeport generally appeared in the swamp during presidential election years, satirizing the circus-like atmosphere of American political campaigns.

The language Kelly created for his swamp friends was especially clever. The cartoonist was an expert at word play. For instance, the beloved Christmas carol "Deck the Halls" saw "boughs of holly" go by the wayside in favor of "Deck the Halls with Boston Charlie." And of course, Pogo Possum came up with one of the great lines in all of Americana when he said, "We have met the enemy and he is us."

MISCHIEF TIME

The great sportswriter and newspaperman Dick Schaap was a friend of Kelly and recounted some of his experiences with the Bridgeport native in his superb memoir, *Flashing before My Eyes.*

Schaap wrote:

> *The great writer John Lardner and his closest friend, Walt Kelly, the creator of the comic strip character Pogo, used to take nitro glycerin pills, for heart conditions. They would lift their pills and say, "Don't anyone move or we'll blow up this place." None was more saddened when Lardner died than Walt Kelly. Kelly was among the handful of geniuses I have known. He drew and wrote a comic strip that had immense political and sociological significance, composed nonsense songs that made incredible sense and authored two of the more memorable lines in the English language: "We have met the enemy and he is us." And "We are the people our parents warned us against." I have rarely been prouder than when Kelly used me as a model for a character in Pogo named Mr. News Life, when he had two swamp creatures invoke my name in the discussion of a football strike and, the ultimate acceptance for his friends, when Kelly drew my name on the stern of a boat drifting through the Okefenokee Swamp.*
>
> *Walt Kelly outlived Lardner by more than a decade, coping gamely and grumpily with heart disease and diabetes. Kelly believed strongly that groaning was good for you. One day, after Kelly lost a leg to diabetes, Jimmy Breslin and I visited him at his home not far from Gracie Mansion, the residence of the Mayor of New York City. Kelly had moved into a bedroom at the front of the first floor brownstone in which he lived. When we walked in, Walt lay on his bed, deliberately exposing his stump. He looked at us and shook his head. "I can't do anything. I can't get up. I can't walk. I can't go anywhere. Until it grows back."*

Walt Kelly died far too young at age sixty in 1973.

Nine Votes End an Era

Hugh Curran, who had served as Mayor Tedesco's city attorney, was elected to replace his former boss in 1965. Curran brought a different style of management to the job than his two predecessors, placing social and cultural improvements in the city at the top of his agenda. To that end, two of the major projects of his administration were renovations to the Barnum Museum and the Bridgeport Public Library.

At the rededication of the Barnum Museum, Curran famously said, "Bridgeport, widely known as a center of industry, must also be a center of art and beauty."

Curran also helped pay tribute to the late Jasper McLevy on November 1, 1967, when the old city hall was rechristened McLevy Hall. This was the same building where Abraham Lincoln spoke to that wildly enthusiastic throng in 1860. Vida McLevy Parsons was on hand for the celebration, which included the unveiling of the official portrait of her husband.

Curran was elected to three terms in his own right, but as he was leading the city, there were stirrings in the long-dormant Republican camp. A Republican registration drive led by Republican maverick James Stapleton spurred a radical increase in Bridgeport Republicans. Stapleton was at war with Ed Sandula for control of the party and wanted to seize control from the longtime boss.

Stapleton tasted success when his faction's candidate, Nicholas Panuzio, defeated Sandula's handpicked candidate in the 1969 Republican primary. Curran clobbered Panuzio in the general election, but that didn't matter as Stapleton and company were just getting started.

Their next step was to try to knock out Republican town chairman George Ganim, a Sandula loyalist. Stapleton selected himself to run against Ganim, and both men knew the race for the chairman's seat was going to be a nail-biter. It was. Stapleton won by a single vote, and the Park City GOP had fresh leadership.

Suddenly, the Republicans were invigorated. Thanks to Stapleton, they had new organization, and they had a viable candidate in Panuzio. However, the Bridgeport GOP had a problem: Curran was popular, and there was no unifying issue for the party to draw voters' attention to—until Curran gave them an issue.

Bridgeport faced a deficit in 1971, and Curran surprised the citizenry by attempting to solve the problem by instituting what he termed a mini-tax. To Park City residents, though, a tax is a tax is a tax, no matter what you call it. The Republicans seized the tax issue, and suddenly, there was a good old-fashioned Bridgeport political battle underway.

This single issue proved to be costly to Curran and the Democrats as their fourteen-year, uninterrupted reign in office was broken with Panuzio's victory. The Republican had won by a whopping 9 votes. The final totals

Right: Nicholas Panuzio became the city's first Republican mayor in forty-two years in 1971. *Courtesy of the Bridgeport History Center, Bridgeport Public Library.*

Below: Change to: Mayor Panuzio (third from left) and future mayoral candidate Charlie Tisdale (second from left) with neighborhood children at the opening of the Mahalia Jackson Community Center. *Courtesy of the Bridgeport History Center, Bridgeport Public Library.*

were 20,535 votes cast for Panuzio while Curran only garnered 20,526. The 1971 contest was the closest election in Bridgeport history.

Panuzio did prove to be an affable and witty mayor, which helped him maintain his popularity with Bridgeport residents. One of Panuzio's earliest triumphs was the Bridgeport Economic Development Corporation (BEDCO), a quasi-public institution designed to encourage new business to set up shop in Bridgeport. Future mayor Bill Finch would one day head BEDCO.

An effective orator who was genuinely well liked, Panuzio tried to roll the dice and aim for the state's highest office, tossing his hat in the ring for the 1974 governor's race. Alas, it was not to be for the gregarious Panuzio, who was defeated in a close Republican primary. Park City voters have noticed that the occupants of the mayor's chair in Bridgeport often gaze lovingly toward the statehouse in Hartford.

One of the moves Panuzio made that endeared him to the Bridgeport Police and Fire Departments but eventually buried the city financially was the so-called 20-and-Out program. This basically said that police and firefighters could retire after twenty years on the job, which meant that from that point on, the city would be paying out a whole lot of pensions and hiring a whole lot of new recruits. This policy is on the books today, and it has proven to be a financial burden for city hall since the day Panuzio enacted it.

Cynics say Panuzio forced through the sweetheart deal to receive the backing of the two powerful unions in Bridgeport in the 1973 election. This would have been a wise political move by Panuzio, but one could argue that trading the city's economic future for a few thousand votes isn't exactly ethical.

Park City voters did not have to worry about such shenanigans in the 1975 election because Panuzio bolted from office toward the end of his second term. He was offered a job in Washington, D.C., with the Ford administration, and he remains in the nation's capital to this day. Under Ford, Panuzio served as deputy administrator of the General Services Administration and commissioner of Public Buildings.

Since his departure from Bridgeport, Panuzio has served as an advisor on urban affairs to President Ronald Reagan and President George H.W. Bush. Mostly he has been a lobbyist, and for years, one of his biggest clients was none other than the City of Bridgeport. The thought was who better to vocalize the city's needs to the powers that be in Washington than the guy who ran the city himself?

William Seres served fifty-five days as mayor of Bridgeport in 1975. *Courtesy of the Bridgeport History Center, Bridgeport Public Library.*

Panuzio obviously is no longer a Bridgeport resident, but he has remained passionately interested in his former hometown. He is on the board of trustees of the University of Bridgeport, has been appointed to several special commissions and is a frequent letter writer to the local media. Current mayor Bill Finch tapped him to head up a special investigative commission looking into the possibility of election fraud in 2010, and he is still held in high esteem by people in the Park City.

By city charter, the president of the common council automatically becomes mayor if the current mayor has to leave office, and in 1975, William Seres was leading the council. Seres served fifty-five days as mayor and eventually was elected as a Republican state representative from Bridgeport before trying for the mayoral chair again in 1977.

Panuzio's abrupt departure left the 1975 race completely up in the air, a total crapshoot for both parties. The 1975 election in itself is a great study in urban politics as to how strong organization and effective campaign strategy can prove to be the difference in an election campaign with no clear front-runners. Political pundits often say the best political races to watch are those in which there is no clear leader, no candidate to coronate.

In those instances, anything can happen. And in the case of the 1975 Bridgeport mayoral election, anything did. In this case, what happened was the election of a grocer by the name of John Mandanici.

5
MANDY

Not bad for a kid from the Hollow, huh?
John Mandanici

Born on New Year's Day in 1918, John C. Mandanici was the kid who got the golden ticket. Mandy, as he was affectionately called, rose from managing the A&P in downtown Bridgeport to become the mayor who ruled with an iron fist and, along the way, became one of the most colorful characters in the history of Bridgeport politics.

The Mandanici family was originally from Sicily and settled in Bridgeport in 1908. The future mayor was born in the Hollow and attended Bridgeport Central High School. While a student at Central, Mandanici was a classmate of future Bridgeport Police superintendent Joseph Walsh. In one of the fabulous quirks of history, both men would rise in later years to become two of the most powerful people in Bridgeport.

After graduating from Central, Mandanici got a job as a grocery clerk and launched a career that would last until he entered city hall. There was an A&P market in downtown Bridgeport, and eventually, Mandanici became the store manager. However, Mandanici had always harbored a tremendous interest in Bridgeport and its politics and finally entered the fray.

Having been active in the Democratic Party for years and also having served on the city's zoning board, Mandy was elected to his first citywide office in 1969, when he became the Park City's city clerk, a position that put him on the city's political radar screen.

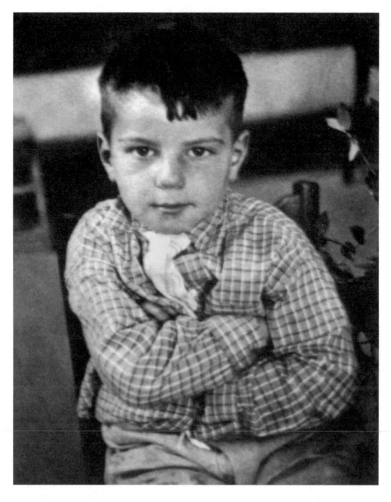

Young John Mandanici. *Courtesy of the Bridgeport History Center, Bridgeport Public Library.*

In defining the role of a city clerk, the eminent political scientist Professor William Bennett Munro, writing in one of the first textbooks on municipal administration, *The Government of American Cities*, stated:

> *No other office in municipal service has so many contacts. It serves the mayor, the city council, the city manager (when there is one), and all administrative departments without exception. All of them call upon it, almost daily, for some service or information. Its work is not spectacular, but it demands versatility, alertness, accuracy, and no end of patience. The*

public does not realize how many loose ends of city administration this office pulls together.

Mandanici used his new notoriety to build up some political capital, and soon he turned his eyes to the mayor's office. The Bridgeport Democrats were ripe for a return to office, especially after the Republican Nick Panuzio had bolted from the Park City for a higher-paying gig in Washington, D.C.

The Democratic regulars were backing William Mullane, but Mandanici had no intention of letting this opportunity pass him by and quickly went to work building his own strong organization. Although the grocer was not the party's officially endorsed candidate in 1975, he flashed his soon-to-be well-known "man of the people" demeanor by telling the party bosses, "Let the people decide."

According to Charlie Coviello, an early supporter of Mandy's, there was a lot more to the upcoming Democratic primary than simply letting the people decide.

"Mandanici cut deals," recalled Coviello. "If you agreed to support him, he'd leave you alone. If not, he was going to go after you, and you would be hurting; you would be on the outside looking in."

Slowly, the endorsements came rolling in. First, former mayor Hugh Curran came on board, and then the unions started embracing Mandy. Among other labor powers, the United Steelworkers of America backed him, and suddenly, Mullane had a serious challenge. When the smoke cleared, Mandanici had not only won the primary to become the Democratic nominee but also wrested control of the party from the powers that be. A new era was on the horizon, but there remained one obstacle in the candidate's path.

Having won the primary, Mandanici squared off against Republican candidate Richard S. Scalo in November. He handily defeated Scalo, winning 63 percent of the vote, and the Democrats were back in office for the first time since Panuzio was elected in 1971. Mandy's six-year reign in the mayor's office was set to begin.

Mandanici wasted little time in solidifying his powerful political organization that firmly controlled the Park City Democrats. The new mayor liked to be seen as the common, everyday Joe who simply wanted to do what was right for his hometown, and that approach was tremendously appealing to many Bridgeport residents.

He was gruff and direct, a political style his constituents found to their liking. However, it also made Mandanici a great many enemies, and his six years in office could easily be characterized as a constant political battleground with his foes as well as his supporters and members of his administration.

A classic Mandanici confrontation took place on October 3, 1928, when the mayor was the guest speaker at a meeting of the Bridgeport Lions Club at the Three Door Restaurant on Madison Avenue. After his talk, the floor was opened for questions and answers, and Mandy happily took all questions, even though the audience had a decidedly Republican bent.

Former mayor William Seres, a member of the Lions, was in the crowd and had refrained from jumping in with a query. Mandanici didn't care and bellowed from the podium, "Go ahead, Bill, ask your question."

When Seres didn't respond, Mandy asked his own question,

Top: John Mandanici dominated Bridgeport politics with his iron-fist rule and common-man touch. *Courtesy of the Bridgeport History Center, Bridgeport Public Library.*

Right: Mayor John Mandanici was a completely hands-on mayor, jumping into every facet of his administration with unbridled passion. *Courtesy of the Bridgeport History Center, Bridgeport Public Library.*

Mayor Mandanici was known as a tough foe and a loyal friend. *Courtesy of the Bridgeport History Center, Bridgeport Public Library.*

"Did you know when you were leaving office you were leaving behind a $2 million deficit?"

At first, Seres didn't answer, but then he mumbled something that not many people could hear. During all of this, Mandanici kept dramatically wagging his finger at Seres and loudly repeating, "Did you know?"

Finally, Seres said, "Of course, John, we all knew."

Satisfied, Mandanici then asked, "Well, what did you do about it?"

Another of the more famous Mandanici anecdotes occurred when he was in a meeting with high-ranking state officials in the ongoing quest to procure more state funding for Bridgeport. Believing Governor Ella Grasso was engaging in two conversations and not paying enough attention to him, Mandy grabbed Grasso's toe, swung her around in her swivel chair and barked, "Hey, lady, I'm talking to you."

Perhaps that type of directness was somewhat offensive to thin-skinned federal officials who launched federal investigations into the Mandanici administration within his first few months in office. This was an ongoing situation for the mayor, who had to deal with federal probes throughout almost the entire duration of his tenure in office. Yet no investigation ever slowed Mandanici down, although the probes became more intense toward the end of his run as mayor.

As *Bridgeport Post* reporter Michael Daly put it, "His administration attracted the FBI like lamb chops attract wolves."

Ironically, Mandanici's biggest antagonist back then was U.S. attorney Richard Blumenthal, who aggressively pursued Mandy and did succeed in indicting a large number of people in his administration. At this writing, Blumenthal is the senior U.S. senator from the state of Connecticut.

Yet Mandanici was quick to point out to every resident of Bridgeport that he had never made so much as a dime other than his salary while he was in office, and indeed, Blumenthal and the feds never were able to secure an indictment against Mandanici. Eventually, nineteen members of the John Mandanici administration were indicted, and sixteen were convicted. Yet the mayor himself walked away after six years in office with a clean slate and an intact reputation.

Mandanici's Teflon capabilities were not accomplished with smoke and mirrors. There has never been any evidence that the man did anything even slightly corrupt during his six years in office, although Blumenthal and company did not fail for lack of trying.

Blumenthal's career skyrocketed in the post-Mandanici years. He became Connecticut attorney general and was elected to the U.S. Senate in 2010 after a contentious battle with billionaire wrestling mogul Linda McMahon. One of the hallmarks of Blumenthal's political style has been going for the limelight. When he was attorney general, barely a week would go by without Blumenthal filing some sort of lawsuit on behalf of the state. The state did indeed become a leader in consumer advocacy, and the future senator received heaps of publicity and plaudits. It is a tactic he has also successfully employed in his current position and one that he began using in pursuit of members of the administration of John Mandanici back in the late 1970s.

The federal corruption probe was a problem Mandanici had to deal with all of his years in office, but it did not soften his charge-ahead political style, a no-holds-barred, my-way-or-the-highway style. Nor was the probe something on which the mayor devoted a great deal of his time. He spent more time figuring out ways to lower Bridgeport taxes and dealing with the daily challenges of the office.

TEACHERS' STRIKE EARNS NATIONAL ATTENTION

One crisis arose in 1978 when a teachers' strike in Bridgeport attracted national attention as more than 260 teachers were jailed. The superintendent of schools at that time was Geraldine Johnson, who was the first black school superintendent in city history and is revered in Bridgeport, where she still resides. An elementary school in the Park City was named in her honor in August 2008. Johnson was named superintendent in 1976, Mandanici's first year in office.

The teachers' union, known as the Bridgeport Education Association (BEA), and the Bridgeport Board of Education were not close to a resolution in their contract talks as the first day of school, September 6, 1978, rapidly approached. Salary was the key issue. The two groups were ordered into mediation, but the talks failed and the teachers walked. The legal problem facing the striking teachers was, at that time, teacher strikes were illegal.

State Superior Court judge James F. Henebry issued a permanent injunction against the Bridgeport strike. He prohibited both sides from commenting on the negotiations and issued fines of $10,000 against the union.

The Bridgeport teachers' strike made national headlines as the days went by, and twenty-two thousand Park City schoolchildren stayed at home. Judge Henebry had had enough after a week. He started jailing strikers and levied fines to the tune of $350 a day against individual teachers. Busloads of Bridgeport educators were shipped to Camp Hartell, a National Guard camp in Windsor Locks that had been transformed into a makeshift prison camp.

Still, the striking teachers and the union showed no signs of folding. The strike continued, and the nation watched.

The first show of compromise occurred on September 22, when the union and the board of education agreed to use binding arbitration to end the strike. Three days later, on September 25, the union voted overwhelmingly to accept the contract, which called for a salary increase of 6 percent in 1978 and 7.5 percent in 1979. The board of education voted unanimously to accept the pact. The city council agreed, and the strike was settled. Judge Henebry immediately ordered the Bridgeport teachers released from jail.

As he left Camp Hartell, BEA president Arthur Pechillo claimed victory, saying, "We have shown the city of Bridgeport, the state of Connecticut and the nation that teachers have the gumption to stand up for their rights."

Through all of this, Mandanici had consistently tried to get the two sides to negotiate in good faith, but the situation was simply too heated. Still, Mandanici was vocal in his attempt to somehow force a resolution to the conflict. On September 20, Mandanici was famously interviewed by Walter Cronkite of CBS *Evening News*. During the interview, the Bridgeport mayor pointed out the national implications of the Park City strike and how the climate needed to be changed to avoid such situations in the future.

Mandy proved to be somewhat prophetic, as the Bridgeport teachers' strike convinced legislators that something had to be done. Clearly, the law declaring teacher strikes illegal was not working.

In the next state legislative session, a new law was enacted in Connecticut. Under the law, the teachers and the school board each choose an arbitrator to represent their interests and the state department of education selects a third, neutral member of the panel. The union and the board then make a last best offer, and the arbitrators choose between them on each issue that has been brought to the table. At the time, the 1979 Connecticut Teachers Collective Bargaining Act was hailed as "landmark" legislation.

Mandanici had cruised to a reelection win in 1977, defeating his old foe William Seres, and was still firmly in control of Bridgeport's dominant Democratic Party. However, the mayor also would extend his sphere of influence to the press, and one of his favorite lines to reporters was "Listen, you, here's how you're going to write this story."

Tim Quinn, a news reporter at WICC radio for nearly four decades, often told audiences that, far and away, the wildest years he ever spent in news were the six years Mandanici was in office. Quinn was part of a group of talented young reporters patrolling city hall during the Mandanici years. Others included Michael Daly, John Gilmore and Jim Callahan. "It was almost as if it were a take-no-prisoners mentality," recalled Gilmore.

INTERLUDE

Bob Crane

WICC, 600 on your AM dial, has long been the voice of Bridgeport and has produced great talent through the years, including the aforementioned Quinn, talk master Tiny Markle, the versatile Tim "Ace" Holleran, Italian House Party guru John LaBarca and the morning team of Mike Bellamy and Tony Reno. But the most famous by far was Bob Crane.

As a morning DJ in Bridgeport, Crane soon was hosting one of the most popular shows in the tri-state area. He was an avid and talented drummer with a keen wit and displayed both skills on Bridgeport airwaves. Crane was scooped up in 1958 by KMX in Los Angeles, and he quickly had the number-one morning show in Los Angeles, adding celebrity interviews to his already popular mix. His moniker in those days was "King of the Los Angeles Airwaves."

Crane was eventually tapped for a guest shot as Harry Rogers on *The Dick Van Dyke Show*, which led him to the role of neighbor Dr. Dave Kelsey on *The Donna Reed Show*. In 1965, he was given the part for which he is best, and almost exclusively, known today—Colonel Robert Hogan in the CBS sitcom *Hogan's Heroes*.

Hogan's Heroes ran from 1965 to 1971 and still remains extremely popular in syndication. It is an unlikely comedy, set in a Nazi Germany concentration camp. Yet it worked because the Allies, led by crafty Colonel Hogan, never failed to get the best of the bumbling Nazis. True to form, Crane not only glibly handled the lead role but also played the drums on the show's theme song.

All good things must come to an end, and so it was with *Hogan's Heroes*. Colonel Klink, Sergeant Schultz Hogan and the rest of their buddies rode off into the land of reruns. But in real life, what was Bob Crane going to do now?

After *Hogan's Heroes*, things didn't go so great for Bob Crane. He starred in a pair of long-forgotten Disney movies called *Superdad* and *Gus*, and his own prime-time TV show, *The Bob Crane Show*, bombed and was cancelled after only thirteen episodes. Crane was essentially relegated to guest shots and dinner theater for most of the 1970s.

The former Bridgeport disc jockey did occasionally find time to visit his old WICC haunts and shoot the breeze with his old buddies, and for Crane, it must have felt like the good old days all over again. Mayor John Mandanici sat in on these nostalgia sessions, and the good vibes echoed over the airwaves.

Former WICC disc jockey and *Hogan's Heroes* star Bob Crane (seated, right) joins Mandy (seated, center) for a reunion at his old station. The star was brutally murdered in 1978. *Courtesy of the Bridgeport History Center, Bridgeport Public Library.*

Perhaps the reason Bob Crane was not getting any more lead roles in Hollywood was that people were finding out about his double life. The beloved star was indeed friendly, witty and talented, but he was also driven by a sexual compulsion that ultimately destroyed him. He was a hard-core pornographer who videotaped himself and his many partners, among other things. Crane's intense addiction eventually became his undoing.

It was during one of his dinner theater stints in a long-forgotten play called *Beginners Luck* that the much loved Bridgeport DJ and drummer arrived at his untimely demise. Crane was brutally beaten to death on June 29, 1978. The former Colonel Hogan actor's body was found in a Scottsdale, Arizona apartment covered with blood with a cord tied tightly around his neck. The case remains officially unsolved, although police long suspected his partner in pornography, a man named John Carpenter, of being the murderer. Crane's life was the subject of the 2002 biopic *Autofocus* starring Greg Kinnear, and the finger was again pointed at the long-dead Carpenter. At the time of his death, Bob Crane was forty-nine years old.

The Beginning of the End

John Mandanici had held his political machine together with tremendous skill well into his second term as mayor, but eventually, signs of erosion began to appear.

The first sign of cracks in the Mandanici regime appeared when he forced a pay raise for himself through the city council. There were not many taxpayers in Bridgeport who thought Mandanici's $28,000 salary was sufficient, including Mandanici. There weren't a lot of them, though, who felt a 50 percent pay raise for Mandy and thirty-eight of his cronies was at all warranted. After the city council approved the raises, the wailing and gnashing of teeth could be heard from a host of Bridgeport taxpayers.

Mandanici's opponents took the mayor and his new $42,000 yearly income to court, where a Bridgeport Superior Court judge agreed that the raises were indeed illegal. Mandy displayed his typical brashness and took the case all the way to the state Supreme Court. In September 1979, the Supreme Court ruled that the raises were, in fact, legal and Bridgeport's mayor had the victory. Or had he? In the end, it would turn out to be a pyrrhic victory at best.

All along, Mandanici said his goal was to modernize the mayor's salary along with those of many other municipal positions. And if he got a few extra bucks in the deal, then so what? Mandy was a guy who had been pushing the envelope for a long time, but maybe this time, he had pushed a little too hard.

In 1980, halfway through his third term, the federal pressure also began to increase quite a bit. Blumenthal and company were turning up the heat, and the first list of twenty-three indictments was released. Mandanici himself had to testify before the grand jury, and he repeatedly took the Fifth Amendment, a move that was legally sound but also would come back to haunt him. Mandanici still had powerful armor, but some cracks in that armor were beginning to show. The Bridgeport Republicans were beginning to notice those cracks as well.

The Election of 1981

The wildest election in Park City history, without question, was the 1981 showdown between incumbent mayor John Mandanici and Republican challenger Leonard "Lenny" Paoletta. It was a race between two bombastic politicians with hard-charging styles who did not much care for each other. This matchup was a recipe for great politics.

For years, Mandanici had inspired devotion from his supporters but also a high level of animosity from politicians who were not in his inner circle. Lately, that animosity had begun to seep into the administration as some supporters were becoming disgruntled.

"I told him straight out," said Charlie Coviello, a Park City political activist who had worked for Mandanici, "that he could count on me working against him."

In 1980, Mandanici also lost the critical support of Margaret Morton, who had been a four-term state representative. According to Morton, Mandanici had promised to back her for a state Senate seat in 1980 and reneged. Mandanici backed city tax attorney Sal DiPiano instead. DiPiano was already a state senator when he was appointed to his new position, and Morton did not expect him to keep both jobs.

Morton, who was black, opted to wage a primary against DiPiano, and the showdown became a no-holds-barred shootout. When the smoke cleared, Mandy's man had lost by a mere eight votes, but he had indeed lost. Morton was on her way to becoming the first black woman to serve in the Connecticut State Senate. For Mandanici, it was the first indicator at the ballot box that the bloom was coming off his rose.

The defeat was more than a loss by a candidate backed by the powerful Mandanici. Morton had energized the black electorate, and a whole new group of voters was ready to stick it to Mandy in 1981. As for Morton, she distinguished herself in the senate, serving six terms. She passed away in March 2012 but was quickly honored by the city. Mayor Bill Finch changed the name of city hall annex, the home of most Bridgeport municipal offices, including the mayor's palatial digs, to the Margaret E. Morton Government Center. The testament to Morton was a tremendous honor to her pioneering spirit and was bestowed in a joyful ceremony held on June 23 in the year of her death.

None of this was lost on city Republicans as 1981 beckoned. Paoletta had no problem exploiting the federal corruption probe into the Mandanici administration and gleefully pointed out Mandanici's willingness to plead the Fifth Amendment in front of the grand jury every time the federals called him to the stand.

Even though he was somewhat more vulnerable than he had been in the last three elections, Mandanici still had a powerful political organization, and it was going to work hard and do everything in its power to keep its man in office. In Mandanici's eyes, he was going to win and make people pay for their disloyalty.

The campaign was strewn with a new standard of viciousness, and Mandanici must have felt he was walking around with a bull's-eye on his chest. In fact, Mandanici later revealed that he did indeed wear a bulletproof vest during the high-tensioned political fray, obviously willing to err on the side of caution.

Another piece of driftwood that appeared during the campaign occurred when the mayor was stricken with Bell's palsy, a form of facial paralysis resulting from a dysfunction of the facial nerve causing an inability to control facial muscles on the affected side. Essentially, the condition is most often an exaggerated form of facial tic that carries no lingering problems but is still quite noticeable. The affliction is named after the Scottish physician who discovered it, Charles Bell.

Mandanici's speech was also slightly slurred due to the palsy, and his opponents wasted no time in engaging in a whispering campaign that the incumbent mayor had suffered a stroke, a horrific tactic. Fortunately for Mandy, Bell's palsy often departs as quickly as it arrives, and that was true in his case. Soon, he was back to normal, and the stroke rumors were dispelled.

The stroke rumors were mild compared to what was coming next. The series of events that took place over the summer during the heated campaign are still being talked about on the streets of the Park City today. And once again, Bridgeport made national headlines—not for the last time and certainly not in a good way.

On August 19, Bridgeport Police superintendent Joseph A. Walsh had a clandestine meeting with a local Park City hood named Thomas Marra Jr. Why would Bridgeport's police chief be meeting with a lowlife Bridgeport car thief?

The reason was simple. Working on the premise that Mandanici was indeed corrupt, the feds also determined that Walsh was corrupt as well. And in Marra, they had the perfect person to try to set up the chief. Marra's family owned a garage and held the city contract for towing, which was worth a cool $100,000. The Marras had held it, that is, until Walsh revoked the pact a few months earlier. The authorities figured that if the Marras wanted the towing contract back badly enough, they would be willing to bribe Walsh to get it back. Hence, the FBI chose young Marra for their sting.

They hadn't reckoned with Walsh. The wily veteran policeman had gotten wind of the sting operation and decided to turn the tables on the feds.

In the meeting with Marra, Walsh pretended he was all in for the scheme, and Marra went to his trunk to produce an envelope with a $5,000 down payment on the $30,000 payoff.

"Should be five in there, Joe. Why don't you count it?" Marra asked.

"I don't want to count anything. I trust you," answered Walsh.

"Sure?"

Walsh replied, "Now put your hands on the dashboard. You're under arrest for attempted bribery. Put your hands on the dashboard."

A Bridgeport officer found a listening device strapped to Marra's leg and beckoned to the feds with glee, "Whoever you are, come out and join the party."

The superintendent had effectively turned the tables on the sting, and the FBI didn't like the turn of events at all. A confrontation between the feds, who demanded that Walsh release Marra, and the Bridgeport Police Department followed. Walsh won that battle as well, as the Park City cops cuffed Marra and took him off to the hoosegow and into Bridgeport lore.

Walsh became an instant media darling, being interviewed by *Time* and *People* magazines, among others. The superintendent told *People*, "They thought they were dealing with a small town cop. If I was a senile old man they might have had a chance. But anybody who offers Joe Walsh money is crazy." Bridgeport had made the national headlines once again. Walsh came out looking like Elliot Ness while the Park City itself emerged looking like Al Capone's Chicago in the Roaring Twenties. Bridgeport had suffered another black eye.

Obviously, if Walsh had been taken out, it certainly would have been a blow to Mandanici's campaign and, at the very least, would have put Paoletta in the driver's seat. And there is evidence that during the attempted sting, the federal authorities tried a back-handed attempt to snare Mandanici as well.

According to the official transcripts, Marra said, "Joe, I got some money put away. I scraped up some cash. It's money I got. I got to give it back to my uncle. If we got to, you know, go through you, through the Mayor, through somebody."

Walsh quickly cut that attempt off saying, "The Mayor's not involved. I'm the one who runs it."

It seems clear from that exchange that the FBI was expecting Walsh to take the bait and that he might want to include his old school chum Mandy in on the take. Already tipped off, Walsh figured out what was happening and cut any discussion about the mayor short.

Mandanici said, "Our Superintendent certainly was a lot smarter than all those Congressmen and Senators who got caught in Abscam," a reference to the recent bribery scandal that had sent seven U.S. congressmen to prison.

In what was probably the most brutal campaign in Bridgeport political history, Leonard Paoletta unseated Mandanici in 1981. *Courtesy of the Bridgeport History Center, Bridgeport Public Library.*

The mayor also demanded a congressional investigation into the Marra incident and received support from a number of congressmen. When Connecticut senator Christopher Dodd tried to play peacemaker, Mandanici became furious at the man he had vigorously campaigned for a year earlier, saying, "You bastard. You'd milk this son of a bitch for all it was worth if it happened to you."

After the botched sting incident, Mandanici went on the attack, claiming that Paoletta was behind the whole entrapment attempt.

Events soon escalated. Marra's car was firebombed outside Paoletta's headquarters. Bridgeport residents may have been wondering why Marra's car was parked there. After all, he had just been on the national news and revealed to the world as a car thief and government mole. Surely he couldn't be a big GOP donor? Or was he just another Park City thug whose car was firebombed in some unknown dispute that the average citizen would never hear anything about?

Two cars were blown up in front of Mandanici's residence on Funston Street, and Paoletta's house was later burglarized. The mayor began wearing his famous bulletproof vest after receiving death threats on a regular basis. Clearly, Bridgeport politics had spiraled out of control.

Finally, Bridgeport voters went to the polls, and the winner was that GOP upstart Lenny Paoletta, who had captured the office for his chosen party. After the bells and whistles and gnashing of teeth had died down and the smoke had cleared and all clichés were saved for newspaper reporters, Paoletta won the election with a plurality of sixty-four votes. The reign of John Mandanici was over.

SWAN SONG

John Mandanici did not go gently into that good night. Did Bridgeport voters really expect that he would? Mandy threw his hat back in the ring in the 1983 race and was one of about a half dozen Democrats to do so. Charlie Tisdale, a former aide to President Jimmy Carter and head of Bridgeport's Action for Bridgeport Community Development, won the primary, becoming the first African American to win a major party endorsement in the Park City. Tisdale beat out former mayor Mandanici and future mayor Tom Bucci to win the prize. Mandy opted to run as an independent, and Paoletta was up for reelection.

One of the problems for the former mayor was that he no longer had complete control over the Bridgeport Democratic organization that he once enjoyed. Michael Daly noted this in the November 17, 1982 edition of the *Bridgeport Post*, writing, "Democrats close to Mandanici turned on him and blamed him personally for the loss and his Democratic colleagues squeezed him out of his seat on the Democratic State Central Committee."

The 1983 campaign between Paoletta, Tisdale and Mandanici featured three dynamic candidates and engendered great enthusiasm among Bridgeport voters. All three candidates had strong organizations and ran vigorous campaigns. The election may not have featured FBI stings and firebombings, but it did attract a 70 percent turnout rate. Compared with a 14 percent turnout in the 2011 Bridgeport mayoral election, the 1983 turnout seems almost surreal.

In the end, Paoletta was reelected, topping Tisdale by about 1,000 votes and Mandy by about 5,500. Mandanici was not deterred by this loss and ran as an independent again in 1985, but he was not a factor as Bucci defeated Paoletta.

Mandanici's health began to fail in late 1986, and he was in the hospital over Christmas. The former mayor was released in time for his birthday on New Year's Day but was back in the hospital shortly after. He suffered a complete circulatory collapse and passed away on January 7, 1986.

For all the controversy that engulfed John Mandanici during his lifetime, he was given a hero's send-off by the city he loved. All of Bridgeport's newspapers published pages and pages of tributes to Mandy, replete with hundreds of stories about the colorful man.

Sometimes friend, sometimes foe Charlie Tisdale said, "I enjoyed fighting with him. Even when I went to visit him in the hospital he said I should be doing this, this and this."

Pallbearers carry the casket of former Bridgeport mayor John Mandanici, who died on January 7, 1986. *Courtesy of the Bridgeport History Center, Bridgeport Public Library.*

Mayor Tom Bucci and John Mandanici's widow, Grace, unveil a new portrait of the former mayor. *Courtesy of the Bridgeport History Center, Bridgeport Public Library.*

Lenny Paoletta recounted that he had seen Mandy at dinner at a Bridgeport restaurant shortly before he became ill and recalled a warm conversation with his old adversary. He was quite pleased the two were able to put political differences aside.

Reporter Mike Daly remembered talking to Mandanici after he had spent the day escorting Jimmy and Rosalynn Carter around Bridgeport during Carter's failed reelection campaign in 1980.

Mandy smiled and said, "Not bad for a kid from the Hollow, huh?"

Not bad indeed.

6
THE BOSS

I will be back. I don't run when I'm fighting.
Bridgeport superintendent of police Joe Walsh

B ridgeport Police superintendent Joseph A. Walsh, known to most simply as "the Boss" served as the head of the city's police department from March 29, 1961, until his retirement on October 5, 1988. Walsh served as superintendent of police for twenty-seven years, three years longer than Jasper McLevy served as mayor.

Walsh lasted through the tenures of Mayors Tedesco, Curran, Panuzio, Seres, Mandanici, Paoletta and Bucci. He was Bridgeport's answer to J. Edgar Hoover, the constant law enforcement authority figure who stayed in power while chief executives came and went through the Bridgeport City Hall revolving door.

"They all had to put up with him; they had no choice," explained Charlie Coviello. "All except Lenny Paoletta, that is." (There is more on that blood feud later.)

After graduating from Central High School with his buddy John Mandanici, Walsh joined the Army Reserve and also became a police officer in 1941. He was called to active duty, however, and served during World War II. Walsh resumed his position with the police department when the war ended.

Thanks to Jasper McLevy and the new Civil Service system, Walsh went through the ranks, advancing from patrolman to sergeant to lieutenant to captain and finally superintendent.

During his twenty-seven years in office, Walsh was considered an innovator by his peers. He established a number of modernizations in the department, including the Canine Corps, the Tactical Squad and the Mobile Patrol. Walsh also instituted a complete realignment of all major divisions of the department prior to moving to the new Police Headquarters, located at 300 Congress Street, in 1966. Walsh is also credited with establishing a computerized records system that was highly regarded around the state.

Although innovative, Walsh was also extremely tough. Everyone knew who was in charge of the city's police department, including the various occupants of the mayor's office on Golden Hill Street. And Joe Walsh had no problem reminding Bridgeport residents exactly who was in charge.

Walsh enhanced his tough guy image and looked like a hero in front of the entire nation when he thwarted the clumsy sting attempt by the federal authorities in 1981. This would not be the last battle Walsh would face during his final decade in office.

Interlude

Whatever Happened to Tommy Marra?

For Thomas Marra Jr., the dupe that the FBI used in an attempt to lure Walsh, life would only get worse. He was twenty-eight at the time of the Walsh escapade and, despite his family owning a lucrative automotive and towing business, was already a well-known car thief. He would soon graduate to other crimes.

Police determined that Marra was not a car thief who operated alone; rather, he was the head of a highly organized crime ring, and the authorities soon began working to build a case against him. In April 1983, members of the Police Auto Theft Unit began an investigation of Marra after receiving information that Marra had formed a stolen car ring that was sending stolen cars for sale around the country. As part of the probe, detectives began putting pressure on Marra's associates to rat him out. During the early part of that investigation, they met frequently with Marra associates Richard Noel and Daniel Sherman.

Sherman disappeared in November 1983, followed by Noel, who went missing in January 1984. Months earlier, another Marra associate, Paul Rice, twenty-two, had been found shot in the head along Interstate 95 in the

Bronx. At the time, Rice was going to be a key witness against Marra in a federal check forgery case.

The heat on Marra was turned up after an employee of Marra, fifteen-year-old Alex Palmieri also vanished. Marra, the small-time car thief had apparently graduated to mass murder. Police eventually arrested Marra for the murder of Palmieri and hit him with kidnapping charges in Noel's case. Noel's body was never found, and it was impossible for police to charge Marra with his murder. Marra was convicted of both murder and kidnapping and was whisked away to spend most of his adult life behind bars.

WALSH VERSUS PAOLETTA

During the 1981 mayoral contest between Lenny Paoletta and John Mandanici, incumbent Mandanici had no problem spreading the word that he believed it was Paoletta who was behind the whole Joe Walsh charade. When Marra's car was firebombed in front of Paoletta's campaign headquarters, it seemed Mandanici may have been correct and was not just adding fuel to the fire.

In any event, there was no love lost between Paoletta and Walsh. He was one of the few Park City mayors who refused to kiss the Boss's ring and made no secret of the fact that he believed Walsh was washed up and over the hill. The battle lines were drawn.

Paoletta made his move on December 15, 1983. Walsh was absent from a city Police Commission meeting that evening, recovering at home from a circulatory problem. Paoletta seized control of the meeting and forced a unanimous vote ousting Walsh.

Paoletta installed Thomas Thear, a former police chief from Battle Creek, Michigan, to take his place. Thear had been part of a team of consultants that had been sharply critical of Walsh and the manner in which he managed his department.

That night, the mayor went on the radio and announced to Bridgeport Police officers, "Attention all police. Superintendent Walsh has been retired tonight. I am the chief law enforcement officer. Take your orders in the normal chain of command."

Given the time of year, Mr. Paoletta apparently wanted to ensure that Mr. Walsh did not have a Merry Christmas.

Bridgeport Civil Service chief Joe Walsh (left) fighting for his job before the Police Commission. Mayor Leonard Paoletta (right) was attempting to force Walsh from office. *Courtesy of the Bridgeport History Center, Bridgeport Public Library.*

Paoletta then made the unusual move of hiring a team of private security guards to protect himself and the Park City police commissioners. Paoletta explained later that it was a precautionary move in case emotions ran amok, apparently believing that Walsh was ready to release a private army of Bridgeport gendarmes to throttle the mayor and restore the Boss to his rightful position at the helm of the Bridgeport police force.

That same evening, the Boss was reached at home by Richard L. Madden of the *New York Times*. As Walsh explained to Madden, "I will be back. I don't run when I'm fighting."

Walsh was true to his word. The Boss brought his case to the city's Civil Service Commission (again owing a good deal of thanks to the late Jasper McLevy), claiming age discrimination. Walsh also claimed that the mayor and his lackeys on the Police Commission did not have the legal authority to fire him. He also pointed out that he had no intention of retiring at this time.

Supporters of Joe Walsh apparently believed the chief should have been ticketed for a higher office. *Courtesy of the Bridgeport History Center, Bridgeport Public Library.*

On January 11, 1984, the Civil Service Commission agreed with Walsh, reinstating him to his position as superintendent of the Bridgeport Police Department. The Boss prepared to assume his old job and headed for police headquarters on Congress Street.

Paoletta was having none of it. He ordered armed police officers to block Walsh from entering the building and berated Walsh, saying, "I'm in charge of this department by charter, and I'm ordering you not to return to this office or this command."

Walsh exited and was greeted by more than fifty cheering supporters outside police headquarters. The Boss told them, "I'm a professional and I take orders. But I'll be back."

The irresistible force had met the immovable object, and Joe Walsh and Lenny Paoletta were headed for a showdown in court.

Mayor Paoletta quickly filed 185 charges of civil misconduct against Walsh in Connecticut State Superior Court, but Paoletta's actions proved fruitless in the end. Judge Robert I. Berdon ordered the Boss reinstated to his position as superintendent of police, saying, "I expect all parties to cooperate and commence a dialogue to settle this matter entirely."

Cooperation was not to be, as Walsh still harbored strong resentment toward Paoletta and the Police Commission, and Paoletta was determined to use his power as mayor to thwart Walsh at every turn.

Paoletta did not disguise his hostility for the Boss, telling reporters, "He's here. He's here by court order. The confidence I did not have in Joe is certainly not restored by a court decision. We'll see if Joe can work within the parameters the court has set and the board has aggressively seized."

When Walsh returned to work on July 24, 1984, he discovered that he no longer would have his magisterial suite of offices on the third floor of police headquarters and would instead be assigned to a small office on the first floor. The Boss also had to contend with a directive issued by Paoletta that required a written approval by the mayor for all expenditures over fifty dollars.

Walsh, a public relations genius, managed to survive, finally retiring on October 10, 1988, when Thomas Bucci was Bridgeport's mayor. By then, the Boss had logged nearly three decades as Bridgeport's top cop. Bucci did not try to oust Walsh, but he didn't make life easier for the superintendent either. Citing financial reasons, Bucci stripped Walsh of his authority to authorize overtime, turning that power over to the board of police commissioners. Walsh responded by eliminating several foot patrols in high-crime areas, but Bucci ordered them reinstated.

Just days before the superintendent's retirement, the inaugural issue of the *Bridgeport Light* appeared, and its lead editorial demonstrated how far Walsh's reputation had plummeted. In its lead editorial, the *Light* called for the Boss's resignation, saying, "Super Joe has become a sad parody of himself" and pointing out that Walsh had become "increasingly intransigent." The editorial

Protesters outside the Bridgeport Police Department opposed to Mayor Tom Bucci's policy toward the department. *Courtesy of the Bridgeport History Center, Bridgeport Public Library.*

board chided Walsh for using city cops as his own private army and added, "The Bridgeport Police Department, despite a lot of good cops, is an embarrassment."

The Boss was probably best summed up by his pal, Bridgeport attorney Joe Mirsky, who said, "Joe Walsh's greatest attribute was that he was a human being. You either loved him or hated him. There was no in between."

Legendary Park City bartender Jack Prince, who served drinks to cops, politicians and reporters at Prince's and the Broad Street Café for nearly half a century, said, "He was the best. The absolute best."

The Christmas Village Miracle

Not everything that happened during Paoletta's two terms in office were as confrontational as his dealings with Walsh. In fact, he was in office during what has gone down in city history as one of the most heartwarming episodes to ever happen in Bridgeport.

A longstanding Park City Christmas tradition has been the Christmas Village created by the city's Police Athletic League (PAL). The village is a beautiful re-creation of Santa's Village at the North Pole, complete with elves, reindeer and lots and lots of toys. Every Christmas season, thousands of children from Fairfield County and beyond flock to the village to see Santa and feel the magic of Christmas.

Things were no different in December 1982, until the unthinkable happened: an arsonist torched the village, burning it to the ground. Bridgeporters awoke on the morning of December 7 to discover everything was destroyed; the entire Christmas Village was gone. The city was stunned, and both adults and children were devastated. Who could do such a thing?

For Paoletta, that question was secondary to this question: How do we rebuild the village? For starters, the mayor called a meeting of key members of his staff at eleven o'clock in the morning and issued a directive: Let's get this rebuilt and rebuilt quickly—as in immediately.

Paoletta's take-no-prisoners approach to the disaster was certainly admirable, but how practical was it? Was Mayor Paoletta Don Quixote tilting at windmills? Thirty years after the fact, Parks Department deputy director Rick Porto recalled his reaction at the time.

"Yeah, I thought he was crazy," said Porto. "But I said, 'What's the worst that can happen? They can't fault you for trying.'"

Word spread rapidly about the horrific fire and Bridgeport's efforts to rebuild the Christmas Village, and the spirit of the season took over from there. Mike Marella, then a police officer and now a Bridgeport city councilman, was the head of the PAL in 1982 and is still in charge of the organization in 2014. He recalled the scene the morning after Paoletta had issued his "Get It Done" orders.

"The next morning, about six o'clock, it looked like a battle scene," remembered Marella. "People were coming up over the hill. Tools, materials, and there was so much food an army couldn't have eaten it. We had two sheets of plywood on horses. That's sixteen feet long, four feet wide, full of food every day."

Donations poured into the mayor's office from around the country, and volunteers streamed into the city to help with the reconstruction. Within hours, it became clear that no arsonist was going to rob Bridgeport's children of this Christmas treasure. Incredibly, on Sunday, December 12, only five days after the fire, the new Christmas Village was back in business.

The herculean Bridgeport task garnered national attention, and headlines around America praised the Park City's community spirit. The resident of the White House noticed as well. President Ronald Reagan telephoned Paoletta and congratulated all involved for pitching in and making children's dreams come true. At the lighting of the national Christmas tree, Reagan recounted the story to all the nation, saying, "Let me give you one specific example of what the Christmas spirit can do."

Paoletta later recounted his feelings to a *Connecticut Post* reporter, saying, "I will tell you perhaps as long as I live I will always remember that episode as an indication of the very best in human beings."

The rebuilding of the PAL Christmas Village remains one of Bridgeport's finest hours.

After being defeated by Thomas Bucci in his bid for reelection in 1985, Paoletta remained an active member of the Bridgeport community. He remains a practicing attorney and most recently has been the head of the Council of Italian-American Societies of Fairfield County.

However, the former mayor was also the victim of one of the scariest and most dramatic incidents in recent Bridgeport history. While exiting a volunteer dinner at the Holy Rosary Roman Catholic Church School on Bridgeport's East Side on September 17, 1994, Paoletta and two other men—Father Guido Montanaro, the church pastor, and parishioner Frank Matera—were shot. The trio had apparently been caught in the crossfire between two rival groups.

The parishioner and the pastor were treated and released, but the former leader of the Park City had suffered serious injuries.

Bridgeport Hospital's chief of surgery Dr. John MacArthur told the *New York Times*, "When they brought him in here he was bleeding badly, he had no pulse and no blood pressure, and he came about as close to dying as you could."

Happily, Paoletta recovered completely and is still a champion of the city of Bridgeport, but the incident is a stark reminder of how dangerous the Park City was only twenty years ago.

7
BANKRUPTCY

John Guman reached down into the political swamp, and he pulled Tommy Bucci
out of the muck and mud, setting him on firm ground.
Jim Callahan

I f nothing else, the mid-1980s vividly demonstrated that the boom times
of the manufacturing center known as the Arsenal of Democracy, a
thriving downtown, political participation and a proud community were
fading further and further into memory.

Crime was way up, the Park City's downtown was barren, businesses were
closing at an alarming pace and the qualities that made Bridgeport a great
place to live and work were fast disappearing. Much of this had to do with
economics, as those manufacturers who were not driven out of business by a
changing global economy fled the Park City for warmer climes down south
and elsewhere.

Of course, there was no single factor that could be blamed for the
unwelcome change, and no one individual could solve the problems and
challenges suddenly facing the Park City. But that did not mean there were
not those Park City politicians who were willing to give it a shot.

One of those budding mayoral candidates was a young lawyer named
Tom Bucci, who, on the face of things, did not seem to be an aspiring
politician. Bucci was an assistant city attorney under Mandanici and knew
the ropes at Bridgeport City Hall. He also enjoyed a well-earned reputation
for being hardworking and honest.

In 1983, those were the qualities John T. Guman Jr. was looking for in a mayoral candidate. Guman was the charismatic, cigar-chomping head of the Bridgeport Democratic Town Committee and strongly believed that the local Dems could best achieve success by disassociating themselves from the rough-and-tumble years of the Mandanici administration.

Backed by Guman and a host of party regulars, Bucci entered the fray in a quest for the Democratic nomination. And it was quite a fray indeed, as no candidate was able to achieve a plurality of votes, opening the doors for a volatile Democratic primary. Bucci and Mandanici jumped in, but so did Charlie Tisdale, who had an impressive slate of credentials of his own.

An African American, Tisdale had worked in the administration of President Jimmy Carter and headed up the city's antipoverty agency, Action for Bridgeport Community Development, a position he holds to this day. Black voters in Bridgeport had been energized by Margaret Morton's recent election to the state Senate and actively participated in the primary, allowing Tisdale to walk away victoriously with the Democratic nomination, the first

Charlie Tisdale (far right) became the Park City's first endorsed African American candidate for mayor when he won the 1983 Democratic nomination. *Courtesy of the Bridgeport History Center, Bridgeport Public Library.*

Tom Bucci was elected mayor in 1985 and served until 1989. The city's finances were the biggest problem that the Democrat had to deal with during his four years in office. *Courtesy of the Bridgeport History Center, Bridgeport Public Library.*

African American to do so in Bridgeport history. It was sweet revenge for Tisdale, who had challenged Mandanici to a primary in 1981 and lost.

This time Mandy had the last laugh. Running as an independent, the former mayor garnered ten thousand votes. That was enough to give Paoletta a one-thousand-ballot victory over Tisdale. If Mandanici had stayed out of the race, Tisdale more than likely would have been elected mayor of the Park City.

In 1985, Bucci was back in the mix and secured the Democratic nomination, setting the stage for a mano-a-mano contest with incumbent Paoletta. The low-key Bucci had kept his name in front of voters and also in front of party leaders in the two years since his loss to Tisdale, and the strategy paid off. He had represented the city's Civil Service Commission in its court fight against Paoletta's attempt to oust Joe Walsh, and Bucci was able to defeat Paoletta in the high-profile court battle. Then, he defeated the incumbent at the ballot box, coasting to victory in the 1985 general election.

Bucci's laid-back style of governing was a marked change of pace from the volatile ten years the city enjoyed under John Mandanici and Lenny Paoletta. Yet Bucci was a proactive mayor and set out to tackle the myriad challenges facing him.

Still, there were those who missed the bare-knuckle days of the previous two administrations. *Bridgeport Telegram* city hall reporter Jim Callahan put it this way: "John Guman reached down into the political swamp, and he pulled Tommy Bucci out of the muck and mud, setting

Jim Callahan was one of a host of hungry young reporters working Bridgeport City Hall in the 1970s and '80s. *Courtesy of the Bridgeport History Center, Bridgeport Public Library.*

him on firm ground. Guman then hosed him off, kicked him in the butt and announced to the world: 'Here's our boy!'"

One of Bucci's top priorities was addressing the problem of Father Panik Village, a public housing complex on the East Side of Bridgeport that the mayor referred to as "one of the worst managed housing complexes in the nation." The complex was completely crime ridden by the time Bucci took office and was a central location for the city's drug dealing. There were also several homicides each year at Father Panik Village.

In a way, Father Panik Village was the perfect symbol for Bridgeport's decline. At the groundbreaking for the complex in 1939, Father Stephen Panik himself described the future housing complex as "the greatest Christmas present Bridgeport has ever received."

Congressman Albert Austin, Mayor Jasper McLevy and Governor Wilbur Cross all attended the ceremony, and Cross declared, "The new village will take boys and girls off the streets and into the playgrounds. Good housing open to sunlight and fresh air and ample play areas are the best preventatives against disease and crime."

Father Panik was a native of Slovakia, pastor of Bridgeport's Saints Cyril and Methodius Church and a vigorous public housing advocate. After years of trying, Father Panik was finally able to persuade McLevy to get on board with the project, as the old tightwad mayor had always been loath to accept federal dollars into Bridgeport coffers. However, in this case, McLevy was able to see the greater good.

Father Panik was named the first chairman of the Bridgeport Housing Authority by McLevy but thankfully did not live to see his beloved housing village fall into ruin. He died in 1953, long before Tom Bucci had to deal with the decaying housing project.

Bucci acted quickly to rid the city of what had now clearly become a slum. The mayor had most of the village razed, leaving only fifteen buildings on the once thriving complex. The remainder was destroyed in 1993, when Joseph P. Ganim was in office, and Ganim noted, "Bridgeport's past plight has been linked to a big extent to the deterioration of public housing and Father Panik Village was by far the most notable example. Its destruction is a very symbolic move."

Not every Bridgeport political observer felt that the city was the only beneficiary of Bucci's actions regarding Father Panik Village, among them reporter Bob Fredericks.

"Developers close to Bucci had bought empty buildings all over the city and converted them to condos," explained Fredericks. "No one was buying the condos. Then the Feds wanted to close down Father Panik Village, and Bridgeport was suddenly sitting on all this money to relocate the Father Panik residents. So they relocated them all to those buildings. The developers made a killing."

Interlude

L'Ambiance Plaza

Mayor Thomas Bucci was enjoying lunch at a Stratford restaurant on April 23, 1987, when he received word that L'Ambiance Plaza had suddenly collapsed. The unforeseen tragedy would eclipse all events in Bridgeport for many weeks to come.

L'Ambiance Plaza was a half-completed residential housing complex in the Hollow section of the city at the corner of Washington Avenue and Coleman Street. Without warning, the structure gave way, and iron- and construction workers were buried under tons of steel and concrete.

With the nation's spotlight once again on Bridgeport, city residents responded with valor, just as they had during the PAL Christmas Village fire five years earlier. The only difference was no lives were at stake in the Christmas Village fire.

Among those who selflessly hurried to the scene of the tragedy was community activist Marilyn Goldstone, who was involved with seemingly every charitable and volunteer organization in Bridgeport. She helped coordinate supplies for the numerous volunteers. There was a pair of "moles," David Wheeler and Tony Tufaro, who slithered into the twisting wreckage in the hopes of discovering survivors. There were none.

When the final heartbreaking toll was tallied, twenty-eight men had been killed, their lives snuffed out in an instant. L'Ambiance Plaza stands as the worst construction tragedy in the history of the state of Connecticut.

In actuality, there were twenty-nine victims, with L'Ambiance claiming Wheeler as its last. The mole never recovered from his experience beneath the wreckage, and his life deteriorated afterward. He struggled with post-traumatic stress disorder and slid into homelessness before dying at the age of forty-six in 2006.

Frank Carroll was the business manager of Local 488 of the International Brotherhood of Electrical Workers and tried to assist Wheeler through his troubles. Carroll finally succeeded in having a stone laid at the foot of the L'Ambiance Memorial at Bridgeport City Hall with the inscription, "David Wheeler, 1960–2006, Hero at a Cost."

As *Connecticut Post* columnist Michael Daly observed, "Though many people forgot about Wheeler in the years after L'Ambiance, Carroll did not. He was the only labor leader to attend his funeral in 2006, the behavior of a stand-up guy."

There were other unexpected heroes in the wake of the tragic building collapse. City attorney Lawrence J. Merly had the unenviable task of dealing with insurance companies in an effort for the city to receive some much-needed funds for cleanup in the wake of the disaster.

Although traditionally insurance has been the biggest industry in Connecticut—there is a reason Hartford is known as the insurance capital of the world—the magnates of that industry characteristically balked at loosening their purse strings despite the enormity of the tragedy.

After sitting through a tense round of discussions with insurance company representatives, Merly emerged from yet another frustrating session and was greeted by a slew of microphones and television news cameras. When asked about the attitudes of the insurance honchos and their willingness to underwrite Bridgeport's cost of the cleanup, Merly uttered a response for the ages. Not the sort to mince words, the Bridgeport lawyer did not hesitate and emphatically characterized the insurance companies as "barracudas content to allow the workers to rot in the rubble." Suddenly, Larry Merly himself was national news.

What the insurance companies had failed to understand was that the entire country was watching the episode unfold. L'Ambiance was national news being played out on the television sets of Middle America, and what those viewers saw was an oligopoly of corporate giants placing their profits above the deaths of twenty-eight people and the heartbreak of a city.

The country sided with Merly and Bridgeport, and the insurance companies caved before the waves of negative publicity that suddenly engulfed them. As a result, the insurance corporations uncorked a multimillion-dollar fund to support the city's disaster costs.

"I just walked out of that meeting, and obviously I wasn't pleased," Merly recalled. "There were a slew of reporters waiting and asked me some questions, and I just told them what I thought. When that hit the wires, the insurance companies called me back in, and we talked again. I guess I said the right thing."

The federal government came down hard on a number of companies involved in the construction of L'Ambiance Plaza, leveling a then record total of $5.11 million in fines. John Prendergast, the head of OSHA, held a press conference on October 23, 1987, the six-month anniversary of the building's collapse. In remarks simulcast in the Bridgeport City Council chambers, Prendergast blasted the companies, saying they displayed a "sense of complacency" and "a serious disregard for basic engineering practices."

Four Connecticut congressmen were on hand for the OSHA press conference: Bruce Morrison, Nancy Johnson, Bridgeport congressman Christopher Shays and future Connecticut governor John Rowland, who would eventually become embroiled in his own scandals.

FINANCIAL CHAOS

Bucci was comfortably reelected to office in 1987, and his second term became marked by the complete ruination of Bridgeport's finances, which, after years of teetering on the brink of total collapse, eventually reached the point of no return. For good or ill, Tom Bucci was the man at the head of the municipal government when the bill came due.

In retrospect, pundits have tried to assign blame on the Park City's financial collapse on any number of individuals or reasons, Bucci included, but in reality, there was no sole culprit or cause. The crisis was simply brought on by years of ignoring the problem. While various public officials acted like ostriches with their heads in the sand, their city was sinking deeper and deeper into the morass.

There was no surprise that by Bucci's second term, the city could not follow its own budget and needed some type of financial panacea to help bail itself out. This situation was brought on by dozens of years of financial mismanagement, Nick Panuzio's golden parachute for the police and fire unions, union and vendor contacts, providing expensive social services to the entirety of Fairfield County and a declining tax base. Furthermore, the loss of most of its manufacturing base shifted the majority of the tax burden to residential homeowners who could ill afford to pay.

Opting to be proactive, Bucci enlisted the help of the state to attempt to solve the crisis. The mayor won the relief from the state to the tune of a $60 million loan but at a protracted cost. The state government agreed to bond Bridgeport's accumulated budget deficits, but the tradeoff was the institution of a state-controlled financial review board that would oversee every aspect of the city's budget and expenditures. Bridgeport was bailed out for the moment, but the city was no longer in charge of its own destiny.

The most glaring instance of the state board's management arrived in the form of a 19 percent property tax increase for Bridgeport residents. Needless to say, this tax increase was not well received. Needless to say, Tom Bucci paid the price.

Larry Merly said it best. A staunch admirer of his boss, Merly summed up the inevitable by saying, "When the mayor in Bridgeport raises taxes, the voters will inevitably punch him right in the nose." And that is just where Mayor Tom Bucci took the punch.

ENTER MARY MORAN

Harry Truman once said, "The Great Depression wasn't created by Herbert Hoover; it was created for him." The same could be said for Mary Moran, who succeeded Tom Bucci as mayor and quickly became the face of the city's bout with bankruptcy.

Voters clearly were unhappy with the state of the Park City in 1989. Crime was up, the city streets were dirty, the manufacturing base had long since vanished, mom-and-pop businesses were fleeing the city in droves and, worst of all, the city was in receivership, unable to make a move without the scrutiny of the state financial review board.

Clearly, Bridgeport voters were unhappy with Bucci, but Democrats outnumbered Republicans four to one in 1989. That overwhelming

Mary Moran remains the only woman to be elected mayor of Bridgeport. She is also the last Republican who held the Park City's highest office. *Courtesy of the Bridgeport History Center, Bridgeport Public Library.*

majority did not matter. After surprising former mayor Leonard Paoletta in the Republican primary, Mary Moran came out of nowhere to stun the Democrats. Despite losing the fundraising war to Bucci by a count of $78,000 to $280,000, Moran outpolled Bucci 54 to 40 percent when the votes were tallied. Mary Moran, the Republican wunderkind, had become the first woman elected mayor of Bridgeport.

Campaigning on the theme "Give This Lady a Chance," Moran employed a strong speaking style and repeatedly pounded the incumbent at every turn, successfully tying Bucci to Bridgeport's economic woes. The night of her electoral win, Moran said, "We are a city in receivership. We are very depressed about the dirty streets, the crime and drugs, the high taxes with no services."

Now those problems were all hers.

Moran embraced the task at hand and valiantly attempted to stem the economic tide with a series of cost-cutting measures. However, it was evident that the there was no way the newly elected mayor was going to be able to put the genie back in the bottle.

Mayor Moran hosting a happy group of Park City Ukranians in her city hall office. *Courtesy of the Bridgeport History Center, Bridgeport Public Library.*

Two key components in Mayor Moran's attempts to restore Bridgeport's economic health were concessions from the many municipal unions and aid from the state. Both of those paths proved to be exceptionally rough to navigate.

Union leadership was loath to give back any of the gains it had made over the years, but the biggest problem for the Moran administration was dealing with state officials. In 1991, the state elected Lowell P. Weicker as its eighty-fifth governor, and the new head of state was to prove particularly unsympathetic to Bridgeport's financial problems.

Weicker had been a powerful Republican three-term U.S. senator, until he was defeated for a fourth election try by then Connecticut attorney general Joseph I. Lieberman. Weicker then tried for the governor's chair as an independent, running on a slate labeled "A Connecticut Party." He was elected, defeating two U.S. congressmen—Democrat Bruce Morrison and Republican John Rowland—and assumed the governor's chair in the state capitol.

Moran and her team had numerous meetings with Weicker in 1991, seeking a state bailout of a $12 million budget gap. That gap would eventually grow to $16 million.

"There was no way that Bridgeport's financial troubles in 1991 were Mary Moran's fault," said George Estrada, Moran's supervisor of streets.

"He did not want to hear anything she had to say. To Weicker, it was the city's problem, and that was the long and the short of it. There was no way he was going to bail out Bridgeport. He slammed the door right in Mary's face."

Estrada meant "slammed the door" literally. Moran recalled, "I will never forget Governor Weicker pointing his finger in my face and telling me that I would raise taxes 18 percent. When I reiterated that was not the answer and that I refused to allow our taxpayers to again be the scapegoats to solve this perpetual problem, Governor Weicker asked us to leave his office. This was the same governor who gave us the state income tax shortly after he was elected in 1990."

Feeling she had no recourse left at her disposal, Moran filed for Chapter IX protection in U.S. Bankruptcy Court, garnering national headlines and a *60 Minutes* segment on her beleaguered Bridgeport, which had become the first major city to attempt such a move. The mayor also brought on a plethora of bad press for herself and her closest allies.

Weicker proved to be more of an obstructionist after the bankruptcy filing than he had when he refused to loan Moran the money to bridge the budget gap. He moved in court to block the city's attempt to be declared bankrupt, with his positing argued by Attorney General Richard Blumenthal.

The state financial review board that had been overseeing Bridgeport's troubled finances since 1988 said the mayor's action was illegal. In a meeting in city hall, board members said the city was not really insolvent and said the mayor had no authority to act without its approval. The board authorized Blumenthal to challenge the petition in federal bankruptcy court.

Donald Kirschbaum, the financial review board's executive director, told the *Los Angeles Times*, "The message we need to send is that as far as this state and board are concerned, the city of Bridgeport will not proceed with this bankruptcy filing."

Eventually, the courts sided with Weicker, Blumenthal and the state financial review board, ruling that Bridgeport was indeed solvent, and therefore it would be illegal for the Moran administration to file for bankruptcy. Ironically, the reason given was that there was too much cash on hand in the Bridgeport coffers to be considered bankrupt. There just wasn't enough money to pay any bills.

Moran refused to raise taxes as Weicker wanted and attempted to judiciously lower the deficit through using the city's $25 million cash reserve that Weicker did not want touched. In any event, Bridgeport's credit rating was destroyed, as was Mary Moran's Bridgeport political career.

Moran said:

> *In 1991 when I met with Governor Weicker, there was no discussion in Hartford about amending or eliminating unfunded mandates that cost Bridgeport and other cities millions of dollars each year. No one in public service had the temerity to talk about restructuring debt that can partially be blamed on egregious contracts that were negotiated at a time during which our political leaders never contemplated or considered the financial challenges our state and nation would be facing today. In 1991, the then-newly appointed State Financial Review Board knew that Bridgeport was in bad shape, but no one wanted to step up and admit it.*

Time has been kind to Mary Moran, who is now the tax collector for the town of Trumbull, Bridgeport's neighbor to the north. There are few people

Mayor Mary Moran stands in front of city hall. Moran thought the city's finances could not be brought back without going into bankruptcy. *Courtesy of the Bridgeport History Center, Bridgeport Public Library.*

today who blame her for the city's financial struggles under her watch, saying she clearly inherited the problem. Herbert Hoover has not enjoyed a renaissance to such an extent, but Moran obviously has her supporters in present-day Bridgeport. Court reporter Bob Fredericks is among them and holds Bucci accountable for the disaster.

"Tom Bucci was the reason Bridgeport nearly went bankrupt, not Mary Moran," said Fredericks. "They would hire politically competent people to nice jobs who would raid the treasury, and it didn't matter if they were connected or not."

In the final analysis, Tom Bucci and Mary Moran were the first two mayors to tell Bridgeport citizens that the emperor had no clothes. The financial problems had been percolating for years, but few political leaders wanted to point out the problem and risk their necks politically. Both Bucci and Moran were given the bums' rush out of office and left the city looking for a savior. In this case, the savior was a young Bridgeport attorney named Joe Ganim.

8
JOE GANIM AND BRIDGEPORT'S SALVATION

I really believe that this guy is going to be a breath of fresh air.
Civil Service Commissioner John Fabrizi on
incoming mayor Joe Ganim

Imagine walking into a restaurant in downtown Bridgeport today, sitting down at the bar and exchanging pleasantries with some of these hale fellows well met. Since this is Bridgeport, odds are the topic might be politics, and some of your fellow patrons might be politicians themselves. If the discussion is politics, there is a good chance that former mayor Joe Ganim's name might well be mentioned, and if that happens, the chances are excellent there will be no shortages of opinion in the room about Bridgeport's second-longest-serving mayor.

There are those Park City residents who will tell you Ganim was the best mayor Bridgeport has ever had; others blame him for the city's ruination. In any event, Joe Ganim remains the only Bridgeport chief executive to serve prison time for corruption during his years in office, checking into a federal penitentiary for nearly seven years.

And if you listen to the whispers in that Park City restaurant very closely, you can hear some voices saying that if he wants to run again, Joe Ganim could probably be elected mayor of Bridgeport once more. Why not? Buddy Cianci of Providence pulled it off after emerging from the clink. The only problem with Buddy is that after he was reelected mayor of Providence, he wound up going back to jail. The former Providence mayor had Bridgeport-area ties as a Fairfield University grad, but Cianci rarely finds himself listed in the "Alumni Notes" section of the campus magazine anymore.

Park City politics saw a fresh new face in 1988 as young lawyer Joe Ganim threw his hat in the ring against Lee Samowitz for the state legislative seat in the city's 129th District. It was Ganim's first run for office, but he opened up eyes with an aggressive style and strong organization, losing to Samowitz by only 150 votes.

Having a taste of Bridgeport politics and growing up in a political family, there was little question Ganim would be back in the fray. He was the son of George Ganim, a prominent Park City lawyer who was also a stalwart in the Republican Party, being the right-hand man of

Attorney Joseph P. Ganim shortly before he was elected Bridgeport's mayor in 1991. *Courtesy of the Bridgeport History Center, Bridgeport Public Library.*

legendary GOP boss Ed Sandula. Joe Ganim was nothing if not pragmatic, and he came out of the box as a dyed-in-the-wool Democrat.

According to journalist and political insider Lennie Grimaldi, who became Ganim's closest political advisor, one of the main reasons that Ganim emerged as such a strong candidate in 1991 was that there were few politicians who wanted the grief of being mayor of Bridgeport for the paltry salary of $52,000 a year, hence there was not a lot of strong opposition with which Ganim had to contend. Whatever the reason, Ganim emerged as a political force and city hall was clearly within his reach.

As the endorsed Democratic candidate, Ganim could smell blood in the water like a political shark. The city was hemorrhaging in a sea of red ink, and the newly minted Democratic standard-bearer was ready to make Mary Moran pay the price for daring to try to have the city declared bankrupt. The strategy was successful, as Ganim finished with a nearly 60 to 40 percent plurality at the ballot box, outpolling Moran 15,678 votes to 10,951 votes. The Bridgeport lawyer had become the Park City's

Joe Ganim (facing camera) and his wife, Jennifer, chatting with constituent George Dunbar. *Courtesy of the Bridgeport History Center, Bridgeport Public Library.*

youngest mayor at thirty-two years of age. When Ganim was sworn in as Bridgeport's fiftieth mayor, Moran was surprisingly unable to find time to attend the inauguration.

As Mary Moran headed out the city hall door, much of the harshest criticism hurled in her direction was not about her handling of the city's finances but more about her lack of communication with Bridgeport and state officials.

An ally, Republican state senator Lee Scarpetti of Trumbull, ruefully told Lolita C. Baldor of the *Connecticut Post,* "Mary had so many problems. She was just going to do what she had to do, and she'd do things whenever she wanted to without telling us."

Civil Service commissioner John Fabrizi, a Democrat, opined, "There are many problems that are beyond one's control. But a lot of little things add up. She didn't establish a rapport with state officials who could have helped

Bridgeport. She worked hard, but she didn't have the capability of being able to run the city."

Fabrizi eventually was elected to the city council and became its president. He succeeded Ganim in office, but at the time of the "Boy Mayor's" election, Fabrizi ironically called Joe Ganim "a breath of fresh air."

Ganim hit the ground running. A solid argument could be made that anybody short of Attila the Hun could have beaten Mary Moran in 1991, given the horrific state in which Bridgeport found itself, but Ganim soon made that point moot. He was a proactive chief executive, and he set the wheels in motion from day one of his administration.

One of the new mayor's first moves was to reach out to Governor Weicker and quickly arrange a meeting with Connecticut's head of state. Weicker, who famously told Ganim, "You do your part, we'll do ours," explained that the Park City was a major cog in the Nutmeg State and could not be allowed to be disabled. Of course, this was an entirely different tune than the governor had sung to Mary Moran, but taking the bankruptcy threat off the table could only bolster Connecticut's overall credit rating, which had been Weicker's main concern all along.

"The City of Bridgeport is just too important to the State of Connecticut to continue to exist in chaos. I think Mayor Ganim is the man both to lead the city and to work with the State of Connecticut," said the governor.

Ganim strongly agreed with Moran on the key point that Bridgeport homeowners could not withstand any more tax increases. The mayor considered the city's residential population base already tremendously overtaxed and sought to hold the line on property taxes. He refused to raise taxes but was also left facing the same crippling budgetary issues that Moran and Bucci had faced.

Through the years, Ganim would not only seek to hold the line on property taxes but also attempt to lower taxes. Lowering taxes was a concept that reached back into the days of Jasper McLevy, when Bridgeport was also in dire economic straits. The 1990s posed a different set of problems for the Park City than the 1930s, however. Most of the financial woes in McLevy's day were the direct result of the Great Depression and would eventually be rectified by time and good municipal government.

In Ganim's time, there were more complicated problems, such as how to replace the tax base that vanished once Bridgeport lost its manufacturing businesses and how to create new revenue streams. These were serious challenges that Ganim had to face, and Bridgeporters wanted results immediately. The Arsenal of Democracy was long gone, a moniker now only meaningful in the mists of history.

So Mayor Joseph P. Ganim set out to find new revenues into the city's coffers and keep taxes down. At the same time, he wanted to clean up Bridgeport, reduce crime and improve the city's overall image, which had taken a beating in recent years.

Around this time, a writer was traveling through Connecticut when he observed a couple male college students looking warily around the New Haven bus station. Obviously uncomfortable with his environment, one of the young men said, "I can't believe this. This is a complete hellhole."

Not missing a beat, his friend replied, "If you think this is bad, wait 'til we get to Bridgeport."

The writer never forgot that exchange.

This illustration is a vivid example of the perception of the Park City when Joe Ganim took office, a perception that in some forms still exists to this day. When people thought of Bridgeport, they thought of drugs, crime, bankruptcy and Father Panik Village. Ganim was in office for the final demolition of Bridgeport's most notorious housing project, being on hand when the final fifteen buildings met the fate delivered by the wrecking ball in 1993.

Bridgeport Police chief Thomas Sweeney pointed out the project averaged 4 to 5 homicides a year out of a statewide total of about 150. Sweeney told the *New York Times* that in 1992, drug dealers shot at three police officers assigned to the area, and in a separate incident, dealers fired seventy-six rounds from a semiautomatic weapon, killing one young woman during a drug deal that had gone sour. Father Panik Village's proximity to Interstate 95 also made it an easy drive for suburban drug users, who police said were involved in about 70 percent of the city's drug sales.

"We are delighted to see it go," Sweeney said.

The razing of the Father Panik Village housing complex was a step in the right direction in restoring Bridgeport's image, but it was only one step. Financial solvency had to be a key ingredient to any hope of a Bridgeport revival, and that objective remained in the top slot on Ganim's to-do list.

Selling off city assets soon became a possibility of both raising money and reducing budgetary line items, and Mayor Ganim was not shy about using this strategy. The city sold Beardsley Park to the state for a total of $4.5 million in a move that was a win-win for both parties. The state received the beautiful Frederick Law Olmstead–designed park, and city residents were still able to enjoy its natural splendor overlooking Bunnell's Pond on Bridgeport's Upper East Side.

In 1992, Ganim set in motion a plan to sell Connecticut's only zoo, Beardsley Zoo, located within the confines of Beardsley Park. After numerous legal issues had been resolved, the sale was completed in 1997. The state created the Connecticut Zoological Society, which purchased the zoo for $5.5 million and renamed it Connecticut's Beardsley Zoo. Not only was Bridgeport's treasury $5.5 million fatter, but the city budget was also relieved of the $400,000 annual outlay it cost to operate the facility. In total, the sale of the zoo and the park added up to $10 million for the municipal treasury.

Through innovative moves such as the zoo sale, Ganim was able to slowly halt Bridgeport's decline. He kept his promise of not raising taxes and eventually balanced ten straight budgets without one tax raise. Joe Ganim was also making a name for himself in state and national political circles.

INTERLUDE

Taking a Shot in 1994

Joe Ganim made his first bid, and to date his only bid, for statewide office when he ran for lieutenant governor in 1994.

He took a circuitous route to the ticket, first staging a run for governor. In early December 1993, Ganim announced that he would be a candidate for Connecticut's chief executive, certainly a bold move. The decision to run for the statehouse demonstrated the thirty-four-year-old mayor's brashness and fearlessness. He had won two Bridgeport elections decisively, but he had only been in office slightly more than two years and was relatively unknown across the state; however, in Joe Ganim's opinion, he needed to strike while the iron was hot. In the end, his bid came up short. Seeing the writing on the wall, the Bridgeport mayor threw in the towel in July and backed president of the state senate John B. Larson, the acknowledged Democratic front-runner.

Ganim had made a name for himself by actively pushing the Park City's agenda throughout the state and with his seven-month long run for governor, and as a result, he was able to secure the Democratic nomination as the party's second banana. Having coasted to reelection in 1993, he had also proved the political wherewithal to be a genuine strength on the statewide ticket.

The Bridgeport mayor ran on the gubernatorial ticket with Bill Curry, a former aide to President Bill Clinton. Curry was a surprise candidate for the Dems. Most party insiders felt Larson had the inside track to first place on the ticket, and throughout most of the campaign season, Larson showed

Joe Ganim was the second-longest tenured Bridgeport mayor, serving from his election in 1991 until his federal conviction in 2003. *Courtesy of the Bridgeport History Center, Bridgeport Public Library.*

commanding poll numbers and, at one point, held a two-to-one edge over Curry. Yet Curry's primary challenge prevailed, and he was the man to lead the Democratic ticket in 1994. Curry also declared he had no preference for lieutenant governor, opening the door for Ganim's unanimous selection at the Democratic state convention.

On many levels, Curry and Ganim were not ideal running mates, mixing like oil and water. They disagreed on many issues, particularly on building a casino in Bridgeport. Ganim was easily one of the biggest proponents for bringing casino gambling to the Park City as a cure for Bridgeport's financial ills, but Curry did not see a casino as Bridgeport's panacea and wanted to limit statewide gambling to Connecticut's two Indian reservations, Foxwoods and Mohegan Sun.

Building a casino in Bridgeport became an obsession for city residents during the Ganim years, especially after Las Vegas moguls Steve Wynn and Donald Trump showed interest in the idea. *Connecticut Post* columnist Mike Daly noted that when he was first elected, Ganim often talked about building up the area around Bridgeport Harbor but, after Steve Wynn came to town, he never heard him talk about the harbor again.

Ganim proved to be a strong running mate, but Curry came in second in a three-way race between winner John Rowland and the Lowell Weicker–endorsed lieutenant governor candidate, Eunice Groark. Ganim had no worries, though. He had performed well on the big stage, and he was still in charge of the Nutmeg State's biggest city. Surely there would be many more days ahead in which he could take a shot at a bigger prize than Bridgeport City Hall.

LET THE GOOD TIMES ROLL

The defeat on a statewide stage did little to slow Joe Ganim's accumulation of political power and his overwhelming popularity. Perhaps most importantly, he also demonstrated a tremendous ability to raise funds, the most important attribute of a successful politician.

In his aborted gubernatorial campaign, Ganim raised an impressive $531,784, a figure that raised eyebrows among the state's Democratic elite and possibly a key factor in why the Park City's head honcho was able to secure the lieutenant governor slot by unanimous acclamation. In news that proved to be somewhat of an omen, there were grumblings from several quarters that the mayor was not shy about using strong-arm tactics to raise a little political coin. It was also revealed that the Ganim campaign had secured $22,500 from United Properties, a Fairfield developer. That particular company would play a huge role in both Ganim's and Bridgeport's near futures, but in 1994, hardly anyone noticed.

In any event, Mayor Ganim had proven that he was more than just a two-term Bridgeport mayor. He was now an established powerhouse on the state level and a dynamic fundraiser. In the mid-1990s, Ganim's political future appeared limitless, and there were no signs whatsoever that his momentum would slow down. The mayor's fundraising ability alone made him one of the most powerful Democrats in the state of Connecticut. Ganim's newly found statewide power base also meant that for the first time in recent memory,

One of Ganim's strengths was reaching out to his predecessors. Here, he is pictured with Mayor Paoletta (standing, right of Ganim), as well as (seated, left to right) Mayors Panuzio, Bucci and Moran. *Courtesy of the Bridgeport History Center, Bridgeport Public Library.*

Bridgeport was commanding attention in Hartford, and that attention was turning into dollars to replenish the municipal coffers.

The two-term incumbent used the 1995 mayoral election to demonstrate that he was now absolutely unbeatable in the Park City and that he was firmly in control of the city. His Republican opponent in 1995 was George Comer, a city businessman who attempted to convince Bridgeport voters that Ganim's vision of the future was not in line with what city taxpayers needed or, for that matter, wanted.

The message didn't sell. Comer was soundly trounced by the mayor, who garnered 15,008 votes to Comer's 2,372. Independent candidate Anthony J. Lancia polled 1,348 votes. Clearly, Bridgeport residents liked the direction Ganim was taking the city and were vigorously rallying around his efforts to return the Park City to its halcyon days of yesteryear.

Although the win was a definitive landslide for Ganim, a disturbing trend became evident by the vote totals of 1995. Only 18,728 voters bothered to cast their ballots for Comer, Lancia and the incumbent mayor. Gone were the days when nearly 55,000 Bridgeporters would go to the polls to decide between Jasper McLevy and Sam Tedesco and change the course of the Park City's future. For such a scant turnout in this, the most political of all Connecticut cities, was indeed disturbing. In fact, this is a problem that persists in Bridgeport to this day, and the problem may be due to the one-party rule that has been essentially in effect since Joe Ganim took the oath of office in 1991. Although politics remains the number-one topic of discussion in the Park City, some voters apparently believe that their ballot is essentially meaningless.

Interlude

A Crapshoot for a Casino

In 1995, Bridgeport mayor Joseph Ganim was in the midst of a more than ten-year run of complete invincibility. The fact that he had aggressively tried any and all measures to yank Bridgeport out of the doldrums of the 1970s and '80s had won him a foundation of support that was virtually impregnable. That the mayor had not raised taxes also helped his standing.

This position of strength also allowed Ganim to put forth an issue dear to his heart and dear to the hearts of his constituents: building a luxury resort and casino in the Park City.

The idea of a Bridgeport casino had been bandied about Bridgeport for a long time, but by the mid-'90s, the improbable idea was gaining traction and political legs. The idea of the old manufacturing town becoming a vacation destination and mini-Atlantic City was quickly taking hold, and Joe Ganim was its champion.

A Bridgeport casino had been an issue in the 1994 gubernatorial campaign and had created a bit of tension between Ganim and his running mate, Bill Curry, who was vehemently opposed to such a measure. Publicly, Curry shrugged off the disagreement, noting that members of the same campaign ticket can't be expected to agree on every issue. However, Ganim realized that whatever the outcome in the race, the idea of Bridgeport as a gambling mecca was now being discussed across the state.

Foxwoods, a casino and resort located upstate in Ledyard, Connecticut, had enjoyed tremendous success, and there were many who believed the Nutmeg State had enough residents who would support gambling casinos in more than one location. Ganim was squarely in that camp.

Foxwoods was run by the Mashantucket Pequots and was officially an Indian reservation. Ganim and supporters of building a casino in Bridgeport were backing passage in the state legislature of a bill that would allow gambling in casinos that were not operated by a tribal nation. In March 1995, Bridgeport held a nonbinding referendum asking if voters would support a casino being built in the city. The result was a landslide victory for the casino proponents.

The idea of a Bridgeport casino was viewed as a panacea by most Bridgeport residents, who considered the proposal a no-brainer. They saw the plan as creating a wealth of jobs, exponentially expanding the city's tax base, inspiring a host of ancillary businesses and making Bridgeport a destination travel spot. Having been downtrodden for years, denizens of the Park City had tired of small steps and gains and were looking for a home-run ball. And their mayor was swinging for the fences.

The citywide casino referendum did not go unnoticed by big-time developers who had been eyeballing Bridgeport since the casino idea was first floated. Among them were billionaires Steve Wynn and Donald Trump, as well as the Mashantucket Pequots, who had no objections to building a second casino in the state.

Also supporting the casino initiative was John Rowland, who was elected governor of Connecticut in 1994, despite Ganim's presence on the opposing slate. Rowland was in favor of gambling expansion in general in Connecticut and articulated that position during the campaign. This put the Democratic candidate for lieutenant governor and the Republican gubernatorial candidate in the odd position of being on the same side of a contentious issue.

Either way, the bill was headed for a vote in the legislature with the backing of Ganim and Rowland, nearly all the residents of the state's largest city and a host of other power brokers who wanted the Nutmeg State wide open for casino development.

To the casual observer, the support was so strong that the result of the impending vote seemed like a foregone conclusion. By October, there were two main players in the hunt for rights to build the Bridgeport casino: Mirage Resorts and the Mashantucket Pequots. Jack McGregor, chairman of the Bridgeport Regional Business Council, felt the best way forward was to build two smaller casinos and award both groups a lucrative piece of the pie.

Rowland ultimately selected the homegrown Mashantucket Pequots as his casino operator of choice and reiterated that the legislature had the final say as to whether or not to approve statewide gambling expansion.

Much to the city's dismay, Mayor Ganim and the citizens of Bridgeport soon realized that support for a Bridgeport casino was not as widespread as they had been led to believe. The main opposition to the venture was emanating from Bridgeport's tony neighbors, wealthy towns such as New Canaan, Ridgefield, Darien, Greenwich and Westport. Although these wealthy communities depended on Bridgeport for numerous essential services such as healthcare and trash disposal, they were unwilling to let Bridgeport share in the lucrative Fairfield pie. Gold Coast legislators cited traffic concerns, health issues and even trotted out gambling addiction in an effort to be viewed as sympathetic to substance abuse issues.

The strategy worked. Republicans in the statehouse forced an early vote on the casino bill in November 1995, despite the protestations of Bridgeport state senator Alvin W. Penn, and the Bridgeport casino bill bit the dust. Penn argued that with more time he could have rounded up the necessary support for the bill's passage, but Rowland sat on his hands. The dream of a Park City casino went back to the land of make-believe.

In an ironic twist, G. Michael Brown, the president of Foxwoods, had been booked to speak at the Bridgeport Regional Business Council's annual dinner on December 1. At the gathering of the Park City's leading businessmen, Brown told his audience that despite the defeat in the state legislature, "The tribe is in Bridgeport to stay." Of course, no one in Bridgeport can remember actually seeing Brown inside the city limits after December 1, 1995.

The Bluefish Rises from the Ashes

It was a rare and stunning defeat for Joseph P. Ganim, but despite the disappointment he shared with the rest of the city, the mayor was not about to stop using aggressive action to keep Bridgeport moving forward. Ganim was also not held accountable for the loss of the casino by his constituents, as evidenced by his huge win over Republican challenger Joan Magnuson in the 1997 election. Most Bridgeporters placed the blame for the loss of the dream on Rowland and the city's own neighbors, rendering frosty relationships somewhat frostier.

The loss of the casino vote meant more than saying good-bye to the solution of the problems that a resort would have brought to the community. The death of the plan also meant another chance at serious economic development in Bridgeport had fallen by the wayside. More importantly, the vote dealt a serious blow to waterfront development.

Bridgeport is located on Long Island Sound and boasts a deep-water harbor that was woefully underdeveloped when Ganim took office in 1991. Most likely, Bridgeport possessed the least developed waterfront of any major city on the East Coast. In the mid-1990s, there were some potential projects that the city was backing, but most were trapped in bureaucratic red tape. Among these were a retail and housing complex to be built on the site of the former Carpenter Technology property and the proposed Steel Point complex on the Park City's East End, which promised a marina, yacht club, retail housing, office space and entertainment venues to beleaguered Bridgeport residents. Unfortunately, Steel Point has undergone a series of name changes and has been the bane of Bridgeport mayors both before and after Ganim. Today, it is known as Steelpointe. Perhaps putting the *e* at the end will spur more financing for the decades-old project.

Still there was hope and a fortuitous confluence of events that brought hope, civic pride and significant development to Bridgeport under Ganim's watch.

Governor John Rowland was apparently feeling somewhat obligated to Bridgeport after the casino vote debacle. Having failed to deliver his own party members to the cause, despite being the Republican standard-bearer, Rowland offered the Park City a consolation prize in the form of "Team Bridgeport" money.

Essentially, the Team Bridgeport money was $125 million set aside for Bridgeport development in five $25 million increments. Rowland had earmarked the money in the wake of the casino failure, but he attached a caveat. All nine members of the Bridgeport state delegation had to agree on the purpose for the use of Team Bridgeport funds. If the reps could not unanimously agree on a project to back, the generous offer from the governor would be pulled off the table.

At the time, Rowland quipped, "Frankly, I didn't think they could ever agree on anything."

Ganim was able to give his counterparts in the statehouse a reason for unprecedented agreement. Bridgeport attorney and businessman Jack McGregor and his wife, Mary-Jane Foster, also an attorney, had approached the city with a plan to bring minor-league baseball to the Park City. Joined by Mickey Herbert, a Hall of Fame softball player and the founder of Physicians Health Services, the trio pitched their idea to the city's Economic Development director Michael Freimuth and Mayor Ganim. Their belief was that minor-league baseball would be the catalyst to restore city pride and inject a much-needed economic shot in the arm for Bridgeport.

McGregor's involvement at the outset was certainly not surprising. As chairman of the Bridgeport Regional Business Council, he had been disappointed in the manner in which the proposed casino turned out. But he also boasted an extensive sports background, and the minor-league team he was trying to establish in Bridgeport was not his first professional sports venture. Indeed, he was the founder of the National Hockey League's Pittsburgh Penguins, an expansion team in 1967 that today is one of the storied franchises in NHL history.

Ganim and Freimuth were quickly on board and cast about looking for funds for the project and a location for the stadium that needed to be built to house the team. Ganim tackled the location problem first.

In his haste to become the first Bridgeport casino mogul, Donald Trump had purchased the abandoned Jenkins Valve building as the ideal sport for his envisioned Trump Park City Plaza. Jenkins Valve was yet another once thriving Park City business that had bitten the dust and was standing lonely and forlorn when Trump purchased it. Located on Main Street in the South End, only a stone's throw away from downtown Bridgeport, Ganim thought the property would be ideal for a baseball stadium.

Fortunately for the city, Trump was stuck with a worthless property (or so he thought) and an annual tax bill of $300,000. Trump was not happy about the annual payment to Bridgeport and angrily let the mayor know about, given Ganim the opening he was looking for.

Ganim generously offered to take the Jenkins Valve site off the billionaire's hands. Trump, who was only too happy to be relieved of the annual six-figure tax debt, ceded the site to the city. Trump was free of Bridgeport, and Ganim had a viable location for a new baseball park.

Having hornswoggled one of the best-known men in America, Ganim set his sights on finding the money to finance the proposed $19 million stadium. Thanks to Team Bridgeport funding, the mayor didn't have to look far. Still, $7 million in city taxpayer funds were needed, which meant city council approval.

As Ganim gained more and more political power, the city council became more and more of a rubber stamp, barely raising an eyebrow to a Ganim proposal. Ganim showed up on the councilmen's campaign literature every two years, but other than those photo ops, the interaction between Ganim and city council members was somewhat limited.

To pull off the $7 million approval for the stadium, some arm-twisting was needed. Leading Ganim's battle in the council chambers were Councilmen

One of the greatest achievements of the Ganim administration was the building of the Ballpark at Harbor Yard and the arrival of the Bridgeport Bluefish. Ganim is shown here in 1997 with team founders (from left to right) Mary-Jane Foster, Mickey Herbert and Jack McGregor. *Courtesy of the Bridgeport History Center, Bridgeport Public Library.*

Bill Finch, Mike Marella and Patrick Crossin, who collected the votes ensuring the motion carried.

The funding was now in place, and construction on the stadium started in late 1997. Thanks to the weather phenomenon known as El Niño, Bridgeport enjoyed one of its warmest winters on record, and construction on what became known as the Ballpark at Harbor Yard now began. The park was completed in time for the inaugural season of the Atlantic League of Professional Baseball, and the Bridgeport Bluefish were born. Fittingly, the dedication plaque at the stadium features a big "Thank-You" to El Niño.

Rowland and Ganim were both in attendance for Opening Day, May 21, 1998, and both men shared the duty of throwing out the ceremonial first pitch. The 5,500-seat ballpark was sold out, and the day remains one of the most celebratory in recent Bridgeport history. The Bluefish won the league championship in 1999 and eventually established a minor-league attendance record. The team recently celebrated its fifteenth anniversary in the Park City and is now a firmly established Bridgeport institution.

CRASH AND BURN

The late 1990s were heady times for Joe Ganim. In 1996, *Newsweek* tabbed Park City's head honcho as one of the "Top 25 Mayors to Watch," a tremendous national honor for both Ganim and the city.

Politically, Ganim had used his clout to mount a vigorous campaign to increase the mayor's term in office from two to four years, saving him the trouble of having to concentrate on bothersome reelection campaigns. A referendum was held, and the charter change was passed overwhelmingly.

The Bridgeport Bluefish and their brand-new stadium had become a reality, attracting visitors to Bridgeport from communities throughout Fairfield and New Haven Counties, and there was a tangible feeling that the city had turned a corner.

There were other honors in store as well. A permanent exhibit featuring Bridgeport, Connecticut, was unveiled at the American Museum of Natural History in New York City on February 12, 1999. The exhibit was entitled "Communities in a Changing Nation: The Promise of 19th Century America" and focused on the Wheeler and Wilson Sewing Machine Company.

Ganim wasn't overly concerned with Bridgeport's glorious nineteenth-century industrial past, nor was he content to rest on the laurels of the success of the Ballpark at Harbor Yard. Instead, Ganim went to work on the city's next major project, a ten-thousand-seat multipurpose arena adjacent to the new baseball stadium. The genesis of the project again sprang from the husband-and-wife team of Jack McGregor and Mary-Jane Foster, but it was Ganim who brought the project to fruition.

The funding was easier this time around, thanks to Bridgeport's significantly improved bond rating, as well as the Park City success the mayor could gleefully point to. Through a combination of bonding and state and local funding, the Arena at Harbor Yard, now known as Webster Bank Arena, became the second piece of the Harbor Yard Sports and Entertainment Complex in place in 2001.

The state-of-the-art venue was anchored by two main tenants, the Bridgeport Sound Tigers and Fairfield University. The fledgling Sound Tigers were the farm club of the New York Islanders and a member of the American Hockey League, arguably the second-best hockey league in the world. Fairfield shifted its men's and women's basketball teams from its bucolic suburban campus to downtown Bridgeport, injecting collegiate life into the city. The arena also became home to concerts and numerous other special events that continued to drive a steady stream of traffic into the Park City. In true Bridgeport fashion, the Ringling Bros. and Barnum & Bailey Circus stops at Webster Bank Arena every autumn. What else could one expect in the city that P.T. Barnum keeps watch over?

As Bridgeport approached the dawn of the new millennium, it was in better shape than it had been in a long time. The mayor, while conceding that there was still a great deal of work to be done, was basking in the glory of his accomplishments and getting ready to tackle his next political challenge.

In an off-the-record conversation with the *Bridgeport News*, Ganim confided, "I think you know I have my focus set on 2002," a reference to the next

The Ganim family—Ganim's father, George (far left); mother Josephine (far right); and wife Jennifer (second from right)—in happy times at a White House Christmas party with President Bill Clinton and First Lady Hillary. *Courtesy of the Bridgeport History Center, Bridgeport Public Library.*

election for the governor of Connecticut. This time, the Black Rock resident would not be entering the race as hot-shot upstart—he would be entering the campaign with considerable political clout and a sizeable war chest. And more than likely, he would be entering as the favorite.

Yes, it seemed to be the best of times for Joe Ganim, but it was about to become the worst.

Rumors were rife that the FBI had been quietly investigating the Ganim administration. Ganim, who was known to be a tough politician, otherwise enjoyed a clean image. Suddenly, Bridgeport was abuzz with the possibility that the beloved development projects were tainted. The word on the street was now that the developers that were awarded the contracts had to pay off Joe Ganim if they wanted to do business in Bridgeport. The same *Bridgeport News* editor to whom Ganim had confided his political plans was now receiving phone calls from state representative Bob Keeley that the FBI did indeed have the goods on the city's mayor.

On December 19, 2000, the FBI executed search warrants revealing what had been an extensive but secret investigation into Ganim's affairs. The investigation was now public, and all bets were off about the Bridgeport mayor's political future. Questions were now being asked: Was he guilty? Was Joe Ganim bought off? Is our mayor going to jail?

Ganim's response to all the sudden negative attention was not dissimilar from when he first took the oath of office and Bridgeport was on the brink of bankruptcy. He aggressively charged into his work and, at the same time, ridiculed any allegations that he was in any way on the take.

The problem was, indictments were being filed, and Ganim cronies were rolling over like bowling pins. Contractors, state and city officials, childhood friends of the mayor and others soon began cooperating with the government in a public manner specifically designed to put the heat on Joe Ganim. Local and national headlines blazed with each indictment and development, and Bridgeport was yet again national news.

Much of the attention swirled around United Properties, a Fairfield development firm with long ties to Ganim and a major contributor to his campaigns. United Properties, run by the father-and-son team of Al Lenoci Sr. and Al Lenoci Jr., was a major Bridgeport developer that was particularly interested in developing the Steel Point project and the Father Panik Village site. Allegations were abounding throughout the Park City that the Lenocis had not exactly played fair in securing their contracts.

As the days ticked off the calendar in 2001 and with the run for Connecticut governor long forgotten, Ganim stuck to his guns and loudly professed his innocence, although the mayor admitted he believed he was indeed the target of the probe. The city populace was divided as to Ganim's guilt or innocence, but there was little doubt that he was earnest in declarations of truth.

Veteran radio newsman Tim Quinn said at the time, "Either Joe Ganim is completely innocent, or he is the greatest actor I have ever seen."

Whichever was the case, it was hard for any Ganim loyalist to explain away the indictments, which were admissions of guilt. Even if Mayor Ganim was above the fray and indisputably honest, the city of Bridgeport was overrun with graft and corruption under his watch. Eventually, many of those indicted would plead guilty to racketeering. Many political wags wisecracked, "Hey, how would you like to be a racketeer? Move to Bridgeport!"

The pins kept falling. On August 26, 2001, Fales Trucking Company of Easton, the lone company to plead guilty in the Ganim case, admitted to inflating the tonnage amount of contaminated soil it trucked out of the Harbor Yard site in exchange for work performed at 45 Sailors Lane in the Black Rock section of Bridgeport, the home of the Joseph P. Ganim family. This was the first time Joe Ganim's name was mentioned in court in connection with the investigation. The cost inflation bilked the city to the tune of $104,000.

A few weeks later, on September 7, the first government official pleaded guilty as a result of the federal investigation, but the defendant was not a member of the Ganim administration. Mark Trinkley was a state official, the head of the Bridgeport office of the State Economic and Community Development Department. Trinkley, a Fairfield resident, owned up to securing a $6.5 million grant from United Properties in exchange for $35,000 worth of goods and services.

Three top Ganim aides, Paul Pinto, Lennie Grimaldi and Patrick Coyne, all pleaded guilty and cooperated with the government. Pinto wore a wire for the Feds for a time and described himself as Joe Ganim's "bagman"— the guy through whom the cash and other valuable goods and services were siphoned. Ganim's childhood friend Frank Sullivan also took a plea in the case, copping to paying Pinto $5,000 for brokering a $1 million life insurance policy for the mayor, which was paid for with city funds.

The pressure on the administration was growing in the extreme. On October 20, Al Lenoci Sr. and Jr. pleaded guilty in the case, the ninth and tenth individuals who had admitted to criminal wrongdoing. The Lenocis testified that they were instructed to pay Pinto one dollar for every square foot of property they developed in Bridgeport, with the understanding that some of that money would be forwarded to an unnamed "elected official."

To most Bridgeport residents, it was just a matter of time before the book would be thrown at this elected official.

In an ironic happening, that book was thrown at Joe Ganim on Halloween when he was indicted on twenty-four counts, ranging from mail fraud to racketeering. He was charged with receiving more than $425,000 in cash, meals, tailored suits, jewelry, home landscaping services and bottles of what U.S. attorney John A. Danaher III called "investment-quality wine." The government was prepared to argue that friends and associates of Ganim had paid hundreds of thousands of dollars in consulting fees by developers seeking work in Bridgeport and that the money was allegedly kicked back to the previously unnamed elected official.

Rowland quickly jumped on the feeding frenzy and issued a call for Ganim to resign, but as usual, Ganim was prepared to fight.

Afterward, Ganim looked into a multitude of cameras and reporters' eyes and declared, "I have done nothing wrong. I have not taken one dime as part of any conspiracy. Like you, I have sadly learned that people who were close to me used that relationship for their own gain and, in doing so, betrayed me and betrayed the city of Bridgeport."

The mayor received cheers from his audience that day at city hall, and many admired his feistiness. The next day, the mayor was at the Galaxy Diner in Bridgeport's North End, telling its patrons and the gathered press that he was still their mayor, he was innocent and he was going to do the job he was elected to do. Ganim would later tell the *Bridgeport Banner* that he wouldn't "sit idly by while Paul Pinto and Lennie Grimaldi played their Get Out of Jail Free cards."

Unfortunately for Ganim, his fate would not be played out in the media, where he still had a healthy amount of sympathy. It would be played out in court with U.S. District Court judge Janet Bond Arteton presiding. The trial began in January 2003 in New Haven and held the city's undying attention for the next two months.

Some of the more interesting nuggets that came out at the trial included Frank Sullivan being told by Pinto, "You have to pay to play in Bridgeport." After Sullivan coughed up $5,000, he testified Pinto told him, "You got off easy."

City council president John Fabrizi caused a stir that left reporters scratching their heads and News 12 reporter Gillian Neff nearly apoplectic on the air. Fabrizi had completed his testimony, and the usual throng of reporters was waiting for him outside the federal courthouse. But Fabrizi never appeared. There was only one way out. Where could he go? The clock kept ticking, and deadlines approached; eventually the media left. Then, Fabrizi walked out of the building. He had a friend with an office upstairs, and he simply sat there until the coast was clear and he could walk to his car.

The most riveting testimony may have come from Grimaldi, who spoke about how the kickback scheme got its start. Grimaldi told the court that Ganim had introduced him to Donald Trump, who quickly hired Grimaldi as his public relations guru in Bridgeport. The former newspaperman was eventually pulling down $8,000 a month from Trump, and Ganim became a little envious and wanted in on the deal.

Ganim never admitted to any of this. He continued to proclaim his innocence and finally got his chance to do so in a court of law. At the last minute, in a moment of hubris, the defense abandoned its lengthy witness list and called one lone witness: Joseph P. Ganim. The gambit failed. To borrow Grimaldi's term, Ganim was "filleted" on the stand by federal prosecutor Ron Apter, who chidingly asked the mayor, "So every one of these witnesses this court has heard was lying except for you?"

The jury didn't buy it, and after a week of deliberation, it found Ganim found guilty of sixteen counts of assorted felonies on March 19, 2003. In

Bridgeport businessman Bill Murphy speaking at an event with two soon-to-be indicted public officials, Bridgeport mayor Joe Ganim (left) and Connecticut governor John Rowland (right). *Courtesy of the Bridgeport History Center, Bridgeport Public Library.*

typical Ganim fashion, he did not resign right away, waiting several days before faxing over his letter of resignation to Fabrizi and city clerk Fleeta Hudson. He faced up to 126 years in prison—racketeering, extortion and racketeering conspiracy represented twenty years each—as well as $500,000 in restitution and $4 million in fines. Ganim received 9 years in prison, of which he would ultimately serve 7, on July 1, 2001, and entered federal prison on September 16, 2003. He walked out of Watkinson Halfway House in Hartford on Monday, July 19, 2010.

The story of Joe Ganim is not finished, but his term in office certainly fulfilled the words of Charles Dickens: "It was the best of times, it was the worst of times."

9

THE FABULOUS FABRIZI

I have no idea how you are going to make this book without raising taxes twenty percent.
John Rowland

Fabrizi was called the "Fabulous Fabrizi," "Fabs" and "Johnny Fabs" throughout his tenure as mayor—fabulous in terms of alliteration, anyway. That comes with the territory when the first three letters in your name are F-A-B. Whether he did a fabulous job in office is up to the voters of Bridgeport and the readers of this book to decide. As mayor of the Park City, he was certainly colorful, radiated enthusiasm, loved his job and loved the city. Of those things, there was no doubt. But Fabrizi also became embattled and controversial.

In the end, Joe Ganim finally resigned, sending a one-sentence fax over to Fabrizi. By Bridgeport city charter, this was all that was necessary for Joe Ganim to cede his office. Ganim was headed to jail, and Fabrizi was suddenly in the driver's seat with the keys to city hall in his pocket.

The new Bridgeport chief executive wasted little time in articulating his beliefs as to how the city of Bridgeport should be governed. In a speech to a packed city council chambers shortly after taking office, Fabrizi repeatedly rejected the words of Paul Pinto by hammering home the phrase, "You don't have to pay to play in Bridgeport."

One of his first moves was to take a page from Ganim's book. Fabrizi quickly arranged a meeting with Governor John Rowland in the belief that Bridgeport

Former mayor John Fabrizi at work at his current job as the city's director of Adult Education. *Courtesy Rob Sullivan.*

absolutely needed to enlist Rowland's aid if the city was to get back on the right track. Since Ganim and Rowland basically could not stand each other, the Republican governor was more than happy to work with Fabrizi.

"John wanted to let the governor know that this was indeed a new day in Bridgeport," recalled George Estrada, the director of Public Facilities during the Fabrizi administration. "That there were new ethics regulations in place, that we wanted to go in a different direction. We also needed his help with the budget."

Fabrizi came into office just as the 2003–04 budget was being debated by the city council, and it was the first major issue the new mayor had to face. Fabrizi knew he had to face the problem quickly, for in the words of Estrada, the budget was "a disaster":

> *We sincerely wanted a set of independent eyes to look at the budget proposal. So we brought the proposed budget to Rowland and the head of his Office of Policy and Management and had them looked at it. We met, and they looked at it for an hour and a half; we ate sandwiches and kept working. I was sitting there, and suddenly Rowland looked up and said, "I have no idea how you're going to make this book without raising taxes 20 percent."*

Using a combination of grants, state aid, budget cuts and smoke and mirrors, Fabrizi and his team were able to produce a budget that was, at the least, palatable to Bridgeport taxpayers, thereby averting a Bridgeport financial crisis during his first few months in office.

Fabrizi's elevation to the mayor's office did not go unnoticed by a bevy of Park City politicians who had been biding their time and stifling their ambitions while Ganim blocked their way. Fabrizi now had the advantage of incumbency, but he in no way had a lock on the election. The result was a free-for-all Democratic primary with no fewer than seven candidates, including Fabrizi, angling for the brass ring. Among them were John Guman III, the son of the late Democratic town committee chairman; Charlie Coviello, seeking to recapture some of the power he enjoyed back in the days of John Mandanici; state representative Chris Caruso, a former Democratic town committee chairman who had managed Ganim's early campaigns but, for the last decade, had been Ganim's most vocal opponent; Max Medina, the chairman of the Bridgeport Board of Education; Bob Keeley, the longest-serving state representative in Bridgeport history; and Carl Horton, an African American businessman and newcomer to Park City politics.

The first candidate out of the box was Guman, a city councilman who, along with state senator Bill Finch, state representative Jacqueline Cocco and developer Phil Kuchma, made a name for himself by being a member of the first group of Bridgeport officials to call for Mayor Ganim's resignation. Guman launched a string of radio attack ads early in the primary season, but his candidacy quickly lost steam. He was never again a serious factor.

Keeley added some levity when he kicked off his campaign, declaring, "I'm tired of breaking in new mayors, tired of it. So, I'm going to run." Keeley had some juice and a strong base, but after his initial announcement, his campaign foundered. Plus, he was unable to raise much funding.

Horton looked strong for a while but was unable to master the nuts and bolts of campaigning, failing to qualify for the ballot by not turning in enough signatures. Keeley had some fun with that development. The day after Horton was disqualified, Keeley was holding court in the Broad Street Café with a couple of reporters and Danny Roach, the Black Rock Democratic leader. Horton suddenly appeared, walking in front of the restaurant window, and Keeley yelled, "Hey, Carl! What are you doing, looking for signatures?" Everybody laughed.

In the end, the race came down to Fabrizi, Caruso and Medina with Fabrizi prevailing by a sliver. Keeley polled over one thousand votes for a fourth-place finish but claims he took out at least one of the candidates. "Anyone who would vote for me would probably have voted for Caruso,"

Bridgeport's city hall, where Fabrizi served as city council president. By city charter, he became mayor when Joe Ganim resigned. *Courtesy of the Bridgeport History Center, Bridgeport Public Library.*

explained Keeley. "I get 1,000, 1,500 votes, and Caruso loses by 200. Do the math. That's why Caruso hates me."

Now came the general election in which Fabrizi would run against Republican market owner Rick Torres, who had beaten Adrienne Farrar Houle in the GOP primary. Torres made the argument that given the fact that Joe Ganim was locked away in prison, the entire Democratic Party was corrupt and change was desperately needed. The challenger attempted to paint Fabrizi as part of the same "old boys'" network, but it didn't work, as the incumbent won a hard-fought victory and became mayor in his own right.

Fabrizi remained personally popular as the city tried to come together now that the Ganim scandals were officially closed and a new era had begun. One morning, Fabrizi appeared on WICC radio and announced he had diabetes. Callers bombarded the station with support, telling the man to hang in there, they were praying for him and they were all behind him.

He made the diabetes announcement on Arbor Day 2006, and Bridgeport was squarely behind the mayor as he revealed his illness. After the ceremonial tree planting at city hall, Fabrizi asked a reporter to lunch, and the pair drove to a local brick oven pizza parlor on Madison Avenue. The reporter was amazed as people recognized Fabrizi's car and shouted out their support. They went inside for lunch, where Fabrizi continued to receive goodwill and prayers for his fight against diabetes. He then ordered two calzones, a large Coke and a large bag of M&Ms. The reporter joined in. After lunch, Fabrizi drove the reporter back to his office.

INTERLUDE

Shooting Himself in the Foot

Fabrizi forged a strong relationship with Governor John Rowland (pictured), but that relationship ended when Rowland was shipped off to federal prison. *Courtesy of the Bridgeport History Center, Bridgeport Public Library.*

Fabrizi wasn't in such an ebullient mood a few months later, and his new set of problems, which would have intense political repercussions, were caused by himself.

In June 2006, federal authorities were conducting an investigation into cocaine trafficking in Bridgeport. The investigators used wiretaps on two brothers involved, and Fabrizi's name came up. Juan Marrero told federal agents after his arrest the year before that he was asked by Shawn Fardy, then a member of the Democratic town committee, for cocaine because Fardy told him that Fabrizi was coming over and needed a hit.

The word leaked to the press, and Fabrizi tearfully told another standing-room-only crowd in the Bridgeport City Council Chambers that he had abused cocaine and alcohol while in office and he was sorry. The mayor added that he was now clean and apologized for allowing his personal indiscretions to affect so many people, but he emphasized that in no way had this ever impacted his duties. He wanted to still serve the people of Bridgeport in the job he loved.

"That was a long time ago, and it was obviously something I shouldn't have been doing," Fabrizi said later. "But even so, I knew people would bring it up, and I gave them a chance to do so. But by the time everything broke, those days were long gone."

Fabrizi came out battling, and he found a city willing to forgive him for snorting coke. He offered to be tested any time with the results publicly released and the *Connecticut Post* twice took him up on the offer. Fabrizi was clean both times. The Bridgeport chief executive went on a mini tour of Fairfield communities to promote the city, and he invited Bridgeport's neighbors in the suburbs to get involved in Bridgeport. He visited Rotary Clubs and breakfast meetings in nearly every community in the area and was open to all inquiries about any subject whatsoever, clearly indicating he was willing to take some hardball questions. Very few people asked about his substance-abuse issues.

As the weeks moved passed after his confession, it appeared that Fabrizi had done very little damage to himself politically, much to the chagrin of his opponents such as Caruso and Torres. He soon proved, however, that he could not enjoy success and destroyed himself irreparably shortly after he had been welcomed back into Bridgeport's good graces.

The Election of 2007

As 2007 dawned, John Fabrizi appeared to be in good shape politically and a lock for the Democratic nomination for mayor, which was almost tantamount to being elected. True, he had far more raging battles with the opposition than Joe Ganim ever dreamed of and had to beg for forgiveness after getting caught in a cocaine scandal, but he was likeable and Park City residents seemed to be comfortable in the direction the city was headed. George Estrada commented on the work they were doing to clean up neighborhoods:

> We worked incredibly hard in those days. We achieved a lot, too. Early mornings, late nights—whatever it took. When we took on an initiative to move blight, I remember walking into community meetings in the Hollow and the East End—well, in every neighborhood actually—and

city officials weren't always too popular. I walked in by myself and told them the problem was in the out-of-town landlords from Palm Beach and everywhere else who let their properties in Bridgeport go to hell. The owners didn't care. Usually, the people would just look at me. Then I would start yelling, "Is it fair that your property values go down because of their neglect?" They looked at me like I was crazy, but then they came on board. And we fined the property owners and made it stick. We made them clean up their blight. The owners thought I was crazy, too.

Juan Carlos Camacho was scheduled to appear in court on March 27, 2007, accused of child molestation, a heinous crime. Shortly after court opened, Fabrizi strolled into court to appear as a character witness for Camacho, who was a friend of his son, Michael. Initially, the mayor had sought to give his testimony in a one-on-one session with Judge Patrick Carroll, but he was rebuffed in that attempt.

Fabrizi took the stand, was sworn in and said the following: "Since I've known him for the past two years, he's been extremely respectful in my house. He has been to my home and is friends with my son. I'm not here to speak about the issue at hand. There is nothing that has led me to believe he has broken the law or is so unfit for society during the two years I have known him."

The city went wild. Cocaine was one thing; going to bat for an accused child molester was quite another. Fabrizi's political future was in dire jeopardy at best. Fabrizi issued a statement the next day. In his apology, he weakly tried to deflect blame in the matter, saying, "I never imagined that by addressing the judge, my intentions would be so taken out of context and misinterpreted."

Sacred Heart University Political Science professor Gary Rose opined, "First you have the drug allegations and now this. It is inexplicable behavior. And 24 hours later he is apologizing. You have to worry about his judgment on a range of issues. It is Bridgeport. There seems [*sic*] to be no sanctions. The city's political machine will save him."

As usual, Rose was completely wrong. Wrong about Bridgeport and wrong about the political machine saving him. Fabrizi's grip on the nomination was loosening fast. Eventually, he withdrew his name from consideration and instead accepted a position Bridgeport's director of Adult Education at a six-figure salary. The whole situation still bothers him, though:

It just got away from me. I was trying to do my son a favor, and I thought there was more to the case than was being reported. It wasn't my idea to try and go before the judge on the sly. I did not want to do that, but the lawyers thought it would be the best way. The judge got real pissed at me, and I knew I had some problems. I tried to control the damage, but I couldn't; it just got away from me. It cost me the job I loved and that still rankles me. I should have gone down fighting.

With Fabrizi out of the picture, who would be the Democratic nominee for mayor? Other than the guy presently sitting in the mayor's office, the most popular politician in the Park City was state representative Christopher Caruso. The veteran North End politician took care of his constituents and could bank on their votes. Caruso knew the right side of the issues and possessed a knack for being able to grab headlines. He also was a major thorn in the side of party regulars, and Democratic Town chairman Mario Testa and the rest of the town committee would rather have seen legendary Bridgeport character Charlie the Bum in office than Caruso. But Charlie the Bum had passed away and was not an option.

So who would it be? Into the breach stepped state senator Bill Finch, who had been a city councilman and had once challenged Republican congressman Chris Shays for his seat. Most insiders felt that Finch preferred the legislative side of government, but after meeting with Testa and company, he decided to seek the nomination. He got the nod, becoming the Democrats' endorsed candidate.

The word spread that the committee members had pleaded with Finch to run as a testament to his credibility, but to this day, Fabrizi believes Finch was angling for the mayorship all along.

"I know for a fact that the day after my testimony in court, Bill Finch let it be known to Mario Testa that he would be the ideal compromise candidate," said Fabrizi.

Caruso wasn't rolling over, however. He organized a primary challenge against Finch and had a great deal of momentum thanks to a great number of Bridgeport Democrats who felt disenfranchised by Testa and the town committee.

When he declared his candidacy for the mayor's job at the Lake Forest Clubhouse in the city's North End, Caruso came out swinging. The newly minted candidate told his supporters, "Bridgeport thrives on the vitality of our people, our unwavering commitment to community and doing what's right. But we have also been held back by a small group of power brokers, and an endless string of machine politicians, that have corrupted our government and tarnished our city. We have to demand change for the lies, the cover-ups, the reckless behavior, the mismanagement and the backroom deals that have shrouded our leadership in darkness for decades."

Although he was articulate and opinionated on a host of issues, Caruso was a one-trick pony in 2007, hammering home the sole point of Democratic corruption and talking about virtually nothing else during the campaign. This was risky, as no scandal had ever been attached to his opponent. Finch was articulate as well, and he was speaking to many issues as well as promising a $600 rebate to Bridgeport taxpayers. Finch told the *Bridgeport Banner* that he would be able to provide a rebate through "good management and cutting away waste in government." The $600 rebate never materialized.

The contentiousness between the two candidates did not stop them from ripping Fabrizi when he doled out $138,000 in raises. Finch said, "This is just the kind of action that makes Bridgeport residents skeptical about city government." Caruso chimed in with, "The U.S.S. Fabrizi is sinking and they are grabbing everything on deck."

In the end, Finch was able to carry the Dems by about two hundred votes. It didn't hurt that a major Caruso mail drop intended to arrive at voter's homes the day before the election arrived the day after they went to the polls. Finch then trounced Republican Mike Garrett in the general election and prepared to step into office as his own man.

10

THE CITY COUNCIL AND OTHER CHARACTERS

You can't pay attention to anything the City Council does anymore.
State representative Bob Keeley

E very mayor of Bridgeport has had to work with the Bridgeport City Council, often referred to as the board of aldermen or the common council, just as the council members themselves are referred to as councilmen or aldermen. In the end, it doesn't really matter. The council exists as a key component of municipal government, a function it sometimes fulfills and sometimes does not. The major time of the year the city council is the focus of Bridgeport's attention is when it approves the final city budget. Despite all of the influence that emanates from the mayor's office, ultimately it is the city council that decides whether or not residents' taxes are going up or down.

In the last few decades, the city council has evolved from a rollicking political battlefield on which a donnybrook could break out any moment to a rubber-stamp outfit whose members enjoy the numerous photo opportunities that come with the job more than anything else. Where this august legislative body is headed in the future is anybody's guess.

Ernie Newton, has been around Bridgeport politics a long time, and he still is a major factor in nearly every election in the Park City. Ernest Newton II made major headlines in 1981 when he became the first African American and, at twenty-five, youngest person ever elected to the city council presidency. Like Bill Finch, he, too, was a compromise candidate.

As the council presidency election approached in 1981, two clear candidates emerged for the office. Democrats Thomas Mulligan and Thomas Caco were the clear front-runners, and it was assumed that one of those two gentlemen would soon be wielding the gavel in the common council. Perhaps they were too evenly matched, as neither could gain a plurality. Once it became clear that a stalemate could not be avoided, both Caco and Mulligan threw their support to Newton as the compromise candidate, and Bridgeport history was made.

Newton's ascendency to the head of the city council coincided with Leonard Paoletta's election as mayor of Bridgeport, and the two men formed a solid working relationship. That relationship would come in handy for Newton during the contentious city council presidency election of 1985.

A few weeks prior to the December election, there were four declared candidates for the council presidency: Newton, Mary Bruce, Chris Caruso and Black Rock Republican Peter J. Holecz. Caruso had run a primary against state representative Bob Keeley in 1983, and after Caruso lost, most

Grabbing a gavel, five candidates vying for the city council presidency pose for the cameras. Ernie Newton (far left) was victorious versus (left to right) Chris Caruso, Tim Mulligan, Mary Bruce and Peter Holecz and became the youngest city council president in Bridgeport history. As a state senator, he was indicted for corruption and served time in federal prison. *Courtesy of the Bridgeport History Center, Bridgeport Public Library.*

Bridgeport political observers were predicting a showdown between Caruso and Newton for the city council presidency.

A few days before the election, Mulligan tossed his hat in the ring, and the race was on between four Democrats and one Republican. The makeup of the city council was twelve Democrats and eight Republicans, so individual and party dynamics were clearly in play.

After the first thirty-four ballots, there was no clear winner, but Mulligan was leading the Democrats with seven votes after Bruce had dropped out of the race and switched her support to him. Voting was suspended and taken up at the body's next meeting, but after several more ballots, no one had broken through.

Then, in typical Bridgeport fashion, there was a sudden change. All eight Republicans switched their votes to Newton on the forty-third ballot, and Newton was elected to his third term as president. Apparently, the GOP councilmen had some sort of revelation after the forty-second vote.

The Democrats, led by town chairman John D. Guman Jr., cried foul. "At what price Paoletta?" asked Guman. "What price did you charge Ernie Newton to sell out the blacks?"

Newton shot back that he hadn't seen Guman doing too much work for Charlie Tisdale, who was the party's nominee in 1983, and wondered why Guman had the double standard.

That Ernie Newton and Mayor Paoletta were allies was somewhat surprising in itself. Newton had once famously dismissed the mayor by saying, "Who is Lenny Paoletta, anyway, but John Mandanici with a blow dryer?"

These were the days when the Bridgeport City Council played an important role in municipal government. There was a wide array of colorful characters who brought passion and commitment to the table. There were more than a few brawls on the council floor and also more than a few times that an unfortunate individual had to be rushed to a local hospital after an impassioned moment during a meeting.

In the mid-'90s with Mayor Joseph P. Ganim firmly in control of the city, things began to change. The city council evolved from a mixed bag of politicians to a group that was essentially interchangeable. In the days of two-party rule, when the Democrats held a twelve-to-eight edge on the council over Republicans, the Democrats were split into a host of different factions so that there was almost never a clear-cut consensus on any given issue.

When John Fabrizi became city council president in 1998, he made consensus the order of the day. Fabrizi did not like to see votes come to floor that had not already been decided and, for that matter, decided by

Bob Keeley (far left) is the longest-serving state representative in Bridgeport history. *Courtesy of the Bridgeport History Center, Bridgeport Public Library.*

an overwhelming majority. Although Ganim and Fabrizi were a study in contrasts, the mayor enjoyed the fact that Fabrizi was able to control his chambers so effectively.

State representative Bob Keeley thought that the council was little more than a twenty-member chorus for Joe Ganim.

"You can't pay attention to anything the city council does anymore," Keeley argued. "They are just a mouthpiece for Joe Ganim. They are just a bunch of sheep."

As the century came to a close, Ganim's power in Bridgeport became virtually unchallenged, and there were few members of the city council who would consistently oppose Ganim or the city council president. One such member was Bob Walsh, a Democrat from the Brooklawn section of the Park City who would repeatedly challenge the majority. Walsh was responsible for a great deal of 19-1 and 18-2 votes, and although he was generally on the losing side of those final tallies, Walsh's opinions usually found their way into the local papers.

Another interesting character from the common council during the Ganim/Fabrizi era was a fellow named Alan Stein, who was the lone Republican of the twenty members. Stein had been a Democrat but switched so there would be at least one member of the minority party on the council.

Unfortunately, one night Mr. Stein's house burned down. During the initial investigation, he was asked if he had any enemies and replied, "Maybe Ganim or Fabrizi."

As it turned out, Stein himself was the culprit in the arson, which one Bridgeport firefighter recalled as "being blatantly obvious that this guy torched his own house."

After Stein's arrest, Fabrizi cracked, "I was going to go to court and sit in the first row and keep flicking my lighter at him."

Some of the more notable members of the city council during the era were Josephine "Penny" Covino, who was John Fabrizi's partner on the city council before he became mayor; John Brannelly, who came from a powerful Bridgeport political family; future mayor Bill Finch; and Auden Grogins and Patrick Crossin, who

John Brannelly came from a powerful Bridgeport political family and was a longtime member of the city council. *Courtesy of the Bridgeport History Center, Bridgeport Public Library.*

Josephine "Penny" Covino was future mayor John Fabrizi's partner on the city council from the 134th District. *Courtesy of the Bridgeport History Center, Bridgeport Public Library.*

Former Bridgeport city sheriff Cecil Young is a fixture at city council meetings and has no problem voicing his displeasure. *Courtesy of the Bridgeport History Center, Bridgeport Public Library.*

were two staunch Ganim supporters in Bridgeport's Black Rock neighborhood.

Another constant presence through the years has been Cecil Young, a former Park City city sheriff who has been the council's leading critic for thirty years. Young can be counted on to let his booming voice be heard on any number of matters that he believes the city council is evading. The former cop isn't afraid to use salty language during his rants, and more than one alderman can be seen cringing when Cecil Young steps up to the microphone.

State Shenanigans

There has also been quite a bit of fallout from scandals at the state level that has affected citizens of Bridgeport as well. There have been a lot of accusations from the Park City populace that in the past few decades, many members of the Bridgeport state delegation have not had their constituents' best interest at heart but rather own self-interests.

While it can be argued that this could be the case for many elected officials, in Bridgeport one representative at the statehouse would often have no qualms about scuttling a colleague's bill, even if it would clearly benefit the city. Getting credit was often the key for such duplicity. "Hey, if I don't get some of the glory, this bill isn't getting passed" was more often than not the mentality of the day.

Although, it was in no way scandalous, Edna Garcia, a four-term state representative from the East End of Bridgeport, felt the cold steel of politics in the 2000 election, courtesy of her pal city councilman Lydia Martinez.

Lydia had a great plan: Edna would run for state Senate, moving into the upper chambers in Hartford. Lydia would then run for Edna's seat in the House of Representatives. What could be better? The two friends could be together in the state capitol and double their influence for their low-income neighborhood.

The only problem for Garcia was that she was running a primary against an immensely popular incumbent named Alvin Penn, who was virtually impossible to beat. And Garcia lost to Senator Penn while Martinez won with virtually no opposition. Lydia Martinez was now a state rep, and Garcia was on the outside looking in.

"I can't believe Edna did that," marveled Hector Diaz, who served with Garcia as a state representative. "She had served four terms and was very popular. All she had to do was serve two more years, and she would have qualified for a state pension."

That episode was only typical of Bridgeport political hijinks, however. There were darker episodes on the state level that had serious effects on the Park City.

Throughout his tenure as governor, John Rowland had, for the most part, not done a lot for the city of Bridgeport. He was not a fan of the state delegation as a whole, and he was certainly no fan of Mayor Joe Ganim. When Ganim was convicted,

Edna Garcia served as state representative in the 128th District and lost her seat in a surprising fashion. *Courtesy of the Bridgeport History Center, Bridgeport Public Library.*

John Fabrizi quickly formed an alliance with Rowland, and Bridgeport began receiving more state attention. However, the relationship didn't last long, as Rowland soon found himself in the same situation as Ganim.

In 2003, shortly after being elected to a third term, rumors swirled about Rowland's having work done for free at his weekend residence by state contractors. Other allegations included the governor's buying into businesses shortly before those businesses were awarded state contracts.

After initially denying the allegations, Rowland admitted that he had indeed had free work performed on his residence, including the installation of an elegant hot tub. Rowland resigned as the state's chief executive on July 1, 2004, admitted his guilt in court and eventually served ten months in federal prison.

Closer to home, Ernie Newton's political career was starting to crash and burn. Having been the youngest city council president in Bridgeport history, he then served a lengthy career as a state representative before being elected state senator following a special election after the death of Senator Alvin Penn.

He pleaded guilty in September 2005 to charges of taking a $5,000 bribe, using campaign donations to pay his own expenses and evading federal income taxes by not reporting the money he illegally took. Newton was given a five-year prison term and quickly reentered Park City politics after his release.

Yes, Ganim, Rowland and Newton all had to pay for their crimes, and John Fabrizi eventually paid with his job. Yet somehow, Bridgeport always seems to recover nicely. And in actuality, all four men have picked up the pieces of their lives after their days in federal court and penitentiaries, save for former mayor Fabrizi, who remained very much on the scene after he left office.

11

ONWARD

*Together we are making Bridgeport the cleanest, greenest, safest, most affordable
city, with schools and neighborhoods that improve each year.*
Mayor Bill Finch

B ill Finch has been on the Bridgeport political scene for nearly three
decades. He has run for Congress, served on the city council and as state
senator. Finch was rewarded with the Democratic nomination for mayor,
defeated Chris Caruso in a primary and then knocked off Republican Mike
Garrett to become mayor of the Park City

Finch's mantra was "Together we are making Bridgeport the cleanest,
greenest, safest, most affordable city, with schools and neighborhoods that
improve each year." And Mayor Finch did help Bridgeport live up to its
nickname by significantly increasing its green space.

The new mayor was involved in some controversy right off the bat. A
state senator at the time of his election, Finch invited some early criticism
by hanging on to both jobs after his election. The fact that he was now
drawing two salaries didn't sit well with many people, and Finch was
forced to defend his actions, citing time was needed for a transition for
a new senator.

Lennie Grimaldi—at one time a Finch friend, supporter and political
operative but eventually a sworn opponent—said Finch should have just
told it like it was. "He should have just said, 'I need the money,'" observed
Grimaldi. "He's got a family; people would have understood that."

Bill Finch soon proved to be an active and progressive mayor, not afraid to fight hard for causes he believed in, particularly environmental causes. He initiated a program called BGreen 2020, a sustainability plan for Bridgeport in which he envisioned the Park City being the cleanest and greenest of all U.S. cities and a beacon of environmental activism for the entire country.

Despite being the largest city in the state, Bridgeport has only one train station on the Metro North line, whereas smaller communities, such as neighboring Fairfield, have as many as three railroad stations. To address this incongruity, Finch proposed building a new railroad station, dubbed the Barnum Station, on the city's East Side.

When skeptics informed Finch how long this process would take, if the station got built at all, the mayor replied,

Top: Current Bridgeport mayor Bill Finch. *Courtesy mayor's office.*

Left: Republican nominee Mike Garrett was defeated overwhelmingly by Democrat Bill Finch in the 2007 general election. *Courtesy of the Bridgeport History Center, Bridgeport Public Library.*

"It doesn't matter if I'm not in office when it finally happens. Somebody's got to get the ball rolling."

In 2010, Bridgeport once again came under national scrutiny and set itself up as the nation's punch line for the first time under the Finch administration.

Shortly before the November general election, President Barack Obama visited the Park City to stir up the urban voting base. Obama gave a rousing speech, and shortly after his appearance at Webster Bank Arena, most political pundits predicted a large voter turnout in Bridgeport.

The pundits were right. The voters came out in droves with a 65 percent voter turnout. Unfortunately, the city ran out of ballots. Democratic registrar of Voters Santa Ayala and Republican Joe Borges only ordered twenty thousand ballots, causing a shortage at the polls and chaos for the election. Chris Berman of ESPN even joined in the wisecracking about Bridgeport, joking about the city while giving the football scores the following Monday night.

Finch wasn't happy. He noted there were over seventy thousand registered voters in the city and added, "This is not acceptable and it will never happen again. Do the math. My six-year-old son can do the math."

Ayala said that her office had followed the proper procedure directed by the Connecticut secretary of state's office, but Borges added, "We both apologize to the voters for what happened. It should never have happened. We'll take the blame."

A few weeks later, the television show *Family Guy* took a shot at Bridgeport. In the show, two of the characters—Stewie, a talking

Joe Borges was the Republican registrar of voters during the "Great Bridgeport Ballot ScrewUp," which brought the Park City unwanted national attention. *Courtesy of the Bridgeport History Center, Bridgeport Public Library.*

baby, and Brian, a talking dog—get lost looking for Santa's workshop and stumble on huge factories with billowing smokestacks and Stewie quips, "This can't be Santa's workshop. This looks like Bridgeport, Connecticut."

Moments later, a cartoon Bridgeport resident writes an angry letter, stating, "I'll have you know that Bridgeport is among the world leaders in abandoned buildings, shattered glass, boarded-up windows, wild dogs and gas stations without pumps."

Mayor Finch took the quip good-naturedly, saying he didn't like Stewie's character on the show but it gave him the opportunity to talk about the positive aspects of life in Bridgeport.

In 2011, it appeared that Finch would receive a serious challenge in the Democratic primary from Mary-Jane Foster, one of the founders of the Bridgeport Bluefish. She was a former actress and an attorney and taking her first crack at politics. Foster's support evaporated at the polls, and Finch handily won the primary. The mayor then won the general election against Republican businessman Rick Torres, who is currently the lone Republican on the Bridgeport City Council.

Finch also attempted a power play with the Bridgeport Board of Education, which was somewhat dysfunctional and confrontational. The mayor's plan was to replace the elected board with a state-appointed board. Although he had some support at the state level and an appointed board was sitting for several months, the plan was eventually overturned in court.

The board of education battle has resulted in tremendous animosity between the board and the mayor's office as well as between individual board members. The net result is due to political infighting, the Bridgeport school system suffered greatly.

JOE GANIM, JOHN FABRIZI, ERNIE NEWTON AND THE POLITICS OF REDEMPTION

One veteran observer of Park City politics recently said, "If Joe Gamin, John Mandanici or John Fabrizi were somehow to run for office again, they'd all win. I know Mandy isn't around anymore, but all of them could win because they have enthusiasm and they have a love for Bridgeport. And the voters can see that."

Bridgeport is a forgiving city. That is certainly the case with Joe Ganim, who emerged from seven years in the slammer looking much the same as he did when he was in office. He has been rebuffed in his attempts to regain his law license, but he has been working for his family's law firm.

The ex-mayor also sparked rumors that he might rejoin the hunt for his old job. Ganim gave an interview in 2011 to the *Connecticut Post* that gave fuel to the fire. He later told a reporter that he had been "close" to joining the race.

Ernie Newton was more than close. He emerged from the hoosegow as much of a firebrand as ever. The feisty politician quickly joined Foster's campaign and, the following year, won the Democratic nomination for state senator, stunning the city. Newton lost in a three-way election to current state senator Andres Ayala.

Fabrizi went from city hall to the high-paying job of Bridgeport's director of Adult Education. "It was the job I loved," he said wistfully.

Who knows if any of the three of those guys may still have a large political role to play in the Park City. In Bridgeport, you forgive a lot.

BIBLIOGRAPHY

Books

Barnum, P.T. *The Life of P.T. Barnum, Written by Himself; Including His Golden Rules for Money-Making Brought Up to 1888*. Buffalo, NY: Courier Co., 1888.

Bielawa, Michael J. *Wicked Bridgeport*. Charleston, SC: The History Press, 2012.

Bingham, Harold J. *History of Connecticut*. Vol. 2. New York: Lewis Historical Publishing Company, 1962.

Bucki, Cecelia. *Bridgeport's Socialist New Deal, 1915–1936*. Urbana: University of Illinois Press, 2001.

Burns, Peter F. *Electoral Politics Is Not Enough: Racial and Ethnic Minorities and Urban Politics*. Albany: State University of New York Press, 2006.

Croffut, William Augustus, and John Moses Morris. *The Military History of Connecticut During the War of 1861–1865*. Ledyard, CT: Ledyard Bill, 1868.

Dannenberg, Elsie Nicholas. *The Story of Bridgeport*. Bridgeport, CT: Bridgeport Centennial, Inc., 1936.

Doctorow, E.L. *Ragtime*. New York: Random House, 1975.

Grimaldi, Lennie. *Bridgeport Italian Style*. Bridgeport, CT: Harbor Publications, 1992.

———. *Only in Bridgeport: An Illustrated History of the Park City*. United States of America: Momentum Communications, 2010.

Lehman, Eric D. *Bridgeport: Tales from the Park City*. Charleston, SC: The History Press, 2009.

Munro, William Bennett. *The Government of American Cities*. New York: MacMillan Company, 1916.

BIBLIOGRAPHY

Olmstead, Alan. *Unpublished Olmstead Papers on Jasper McLevy*. Bridgeport History Center, Bridgeport Public Library.

Palmquist, David. *Bridgeport: A Pictorial History*. Norfolk/Virginia Beach: Danning Company Publishers, 1988.

Saxon, A.H. *P.T. Barnum: The Legend and the Man*. New York: Columbia University Press, 1989.

Schaap, Dick. *Flashing before My Eyes*. New York: Harper Collins, 2001.

Twain, Mark. *A Connecticut Yankee in King Arthur's Court*. Cornwall, NY: Dodd, Mead and Company, 1960. Original Printing, 1889.

Waldo, George. *The Standard's History of Bridgeport: The Promise of the Future*. Bridgeport, CT: F.T. Smiley and Company, 1897.

Waldo, George, Jr. *History of Bridgeport and Vicinity*. Vols. 1–2. New York: S.J. Clarke Publishing Company, 1917.

NEWSPAPERS AND MAGAZINES

Boston Globe
Bridgeport Banner
Bridgeport Daily Advertiser and Weekly Farmer
Bridgeport Daily Standards
Bridgeport Evening Post
Bridgeport Evening Standard
Bridgeport Herald
Bridgeport Light
Bridgeport News
Bridgeport Post
Bridgeport Sunday Herald
Bridgeport Telegram
Chicago Sentinel
Chicago Tribune
Connecticut Post
Day of New London
Eugene (OR) Register-Guard
Fairfield County Weekly
Freeport (IL) Journal
Hartford Courant
Hartford Post
Hour of Norwalk
Lewiston (ME) Evening Journal
Los Angeles Times
New Haven Register

BIBLIOGRAPHY

Newsweek
New York Times
Orlando Sentinel
People
Time
Worcester Telegram & Gazette
Yale Daily News

WEBSITES

onlyinbridgeport.com
www.abrahamlincoln'sclassroom.com
www.bobcrane.com
www.bridgeportbanner.com
www.bridgeportct.gov
www.findagrave.com
www.ibew.org
www.millercenter.org
www.presidency.ucsb.edu
www.tvnews.vanderbilt.edu

INTERVIEWS

Tom Bucci
Jim Callahan
Chris Caruso
Charlie Coviello
Mike Daly
George Estrada
John Fabrizi
Bill Finch
Bob Fredericks
John Gilmore
Lennie Grimaldi
Bob Keeley

Max Medina
Larry Merly
Mary Moran
Ernie Newton
Lenny Paoletta
Jack Prince
Tim Quinn
Lee Samowitz
John D. Sullivan
Rick Torres
Cecil Young

ABOUT THE AUTHOR

Rob Sullivan is a veteran Connecticut newspaper reporter and editor and has covered the city of Bridgeport, Connecticut, for nearly two decades. He is currently the executive editor of the *Bridgeport Banner* newspaper and website. An involved member of the Bridgeport community, Rob is a member of the Bridgeport Community Historical Society and is a member of the board of directors of the Friends of the Bridgeport Public Library. He has won numerous journalistic awards and is the inaugural winner of the Bill Gonillo Award for Excellence in Community Sports Writing presented by the Fairfield County Sports Hall of Fame. Rob graduated with a degree in history and politics from Fairfield University and lives in Bridgeport.